IS IT A CHOICE?

Is It a Choice?

The Male Couple's Guide

*Making History: The Struggle for Gay
and Lesbian Equal Rights 1945–1990*

Expect the Worst (You Won't Be Disappointed)

IS IT A CHOICE ?

■ ■ ■

Answers to 300 of the Most
Frequently Asked Questions
About Gays and Lesbians

■ ■ ■

ERIC MARCUS

■ HarperSanFrancisco
A Division of HarperCollins*Publishers*

FIRST EDITION

Library of Congress Cataloging-in-Publication Data
Marcus, Eric.
    Is it a choice? : answers to 300 of the most frequently asked
questions about gays and lesbians / Eric Marcus.
        p.   cm.
    Includes bibliographical references and index.
    ISBN 0–06–250664–1
    1. Homosexuality—United States—Miscellanea.   2. Gay
men—United States—Miscellanea.   3. Lesbians—United
States—Miscellanea.   I. Title.
HQ76.3.U5M35   1993
305.9'0664—dc20
                                                    92–56425
                                                        CIP

98 99 RRD-H 20 19 18 17 16 15 14 13

To Duf, who wasn't afraid to ask.

CONTENTS

ACKNOWLEDGMENTS

Many thanks to my editor, Barbara Moulton, for sharing my enthusiasm for *Is It a Choice?*; Alison Ames, for generously providing a very comfortable place to work; Barry Owen, for his help on the proposal; and Ann Northrop, for her wisdom, encouragement, and support. And special thanks to all those who suggested questions, offered sage advice, and/or read the manuscript, including Lisa Bach, Dr. Betty Berzon, Mark Burstein, Cate Corcoran, Christine Egan, Ilan Greenberg, Cynthia Grossman, Fred Hertz's grandmother, Alex Lash, Aaron Levaco, Peggy Levine, Matthew Lore, Cecilia Marcus, Steven Mazzola, Bill Megevick, Judy Montague, Jessica Morris, Joel Roselin, Phil Roselin, Bill Russell, Stuart Schear, Bill Smith, Scott Terranella, and Nick Wingfield.

INTRODUCTION

In 1988, I traveled to several major U.S. cities to promote my new book, *The Male Couple's Guide.* I thought I was going to talk about the book, which is a basic, practical handbook for gay men covering everything from finding a man and moving in together to managing joint finances and taking a new spouse home to meet the family. Out of nearly a hundred radio, newspaper, and television interviews, I almost never got to talk about these subjects. Instead, interviewers and talk show telephone callers asked, "How do you know you're a homosexual?" "How do parents react to a gay child?" "Why do gay people want to get married?" "Do gay parents raise gay children?" "Who plays the husband, and who plays the wife?" "Why do gay people have to flaunt it?"

I quickly discovered that almost no one asked me questions that related to couple relationships, because most people didn't even understand what a homosexual was. And very often I found myself responding to people who had comments like, "God created Adam and Eve, not Adam and Steve." I never imagined when I wrote a book on couples that I would wind up talking about Leviticus, Paul, and what Jesus had to say about homosexuality.

At first I wondered, Why are they asking me? What did I know? I wasn't an expert. I wasn't a gay rights activist. I wasn't a psychologist. But whether or not I liked it or felt prepared to answer the questions, I was a living, breathing representative of the gay world. It reminded me of when I was an exchange student in Denmark and people would ask me questions about life in the United States or U.S. foreign policy as if I were my country's representative to the Danish government. Here I was cast in the role of an ambassador from the land of the homosexuals. In fact, it was a wonderful unexpected opportunity to help educate people and dispel ancient and destructive myths about gay and lesbian people. So I answered the questions as best I could, and after a while I answered many questions with confidence. At first I prefaced my answers by saying, "I can't speak for all gay people, but I *can* speak for the gay people I've interviewed. . . ." But no one seemed to pay attention to my disclaimer and simply assumed that I spoke for all gay and lesbian people.

Once I realized that I was never going to get to talk about my book, I encouraged my questioners—both the professionals and the telephone callers on radio and TV call-in shows—to ask me whatever they liked. I explained that no question was a stupid question. By the end of the tour, however, I was more than a little frustrated by having to answer the same basic questions over and over again.

One night, at dinner with my good friends Duffie and Simeon, I shared some of my frustrations. I had just come from another radio call-in interview show and said, "You can't believe the stupid questions I have to answer." Duf asked, "What kinds of stupid questions do people ask you?" And I gave a long list, including the one asked most frequently, "Is it a choice?" Duf flushed, paused, and said, "Those don't sound like stupid questions to me." Simeon said, "Isn't it a choice?" I almost fell off my chair. These were my friends. Didn't they know? After all, they had known me for five years, since Duf and I met at graduate school. The fact I was gay had never been an issue. But I realized that we had never really talked about it after the first time I told Duf I was gay. I just assumed they already had the answers. But where would they have got them from, if not from me?

The next week, I had dinner with mutual friends, Kate and Rick. I related what had happened the week before. I got to the point in the story where Duf commented, "Those don't sound like stupid questions," and Kate asked me, "What kinds of questions are people asking?" I told her, and she said, "Those don't sound like stupid questions to me." Again, I was stunned. I knew that most people didn't know much about gay men and lesbians—but my friends? Clearly, I had mistaken assumptions about what people knew.

These two dinners made me realize the need for a book like *Is It a Choice? Answers to 300 of the Most Frequently Asked Questions About Gays and Lesbians.* Four years after I first had the idea for this book, and after writing another couple of books, I found an editor, Barbara Moulton at Harper San Francisco, who shared my conviction that this was a book we all needed—both straight *and* gay people.

So what do I know? A lot. But certainly not enough to ask or answer all the questions in this book. That's why I talked to plenty of other people (including many experts), depended on magazine and newspaper articles, and scanned the pages of many, many books. What I've learned, you'll find in the pages that follow, including all kinds of questions, from the very basic to the extremely specific. In response to these questions, you'll find brief answers, long answers, anecdotes, opinion, and conjecture. More than a few will leave you with more questions, because I've included questions that don't yet have definitive answers.

The answers I offer here are not the only possible answers to these many questions. Other gay and lesbian people would likely answer these questions differently because gay men and women are a diverse population with different values and different ways of looking at our world.

Some people will be disappointed to discover in the answers I offer that gay men and lesbians aren't nearly as exotic as they thought they were. In fact, some gay and lesbian people *are* pretty exotic, as are some heterosexual people. But in writing a general question-and-answer book like *Is It a Choice?* I stuck pretty close to the broad middle of lesbian and gay life.

You'll meet all kinds of people in *Is It a Choice?* Some give answers to questions; others provide stories that help support a point. When I've used quotes or anecdotes from experts and public people, like gay and lesbian rights activists, I used complete names. When I've quoted private citizens or used their anecdotes—some of which are composites drawn from several different people—I've used only first names to protect the privacy of the people I'm quoting.

Is It a Choice? includes more than three hundred questions; but not all the possible questions are here, nor are all the answers. If there's a question I've missed that you'd like answered, or if you have an answer to a question that I either didn't have an answer for or that you feel I didn't answer adequately, write to me at my publisher. And remember, there really is no such thing as a stupid question.

Eric Marcus
c/o Harper San Francisco
1160 Battery Street
San Francisco, CA 94111

"There's no such thing as a stupid question."

1

THE BASICS

▪ What is a homosexual?

A homosexual person is a man or woman whose feelings of sexual attraction are for someone of the same sex. The word *homosexual* was first used by Karl Maria Kertbeny in an 1869 pamphlet in which he argued for the repeal of Prussia's antihomosexual laws. *Homosexual* combines the Greek word for "same" with the Latin word for "sex." In contrast, a heterosexual is a man or woman whose feelings of sexual attraction are for the opposite sex.

Homosexual people come in all shapes and sizes and from all walks of life, just like heterosexual people do. Some are single, and some are involved in long-term, loving relationships with same-sex partners. Some have children and grandchildren, others don't. Homosexual people are a part of every community and every family, which means that everyone knows someone who is homosexual. Most people just don't realize that they know, and perhaps love, someone who is homosexual, because many—if not most—homosexuals keep their sexual orientation a secret.

I wish I had known what a homosexual was when I was growing up. At first I didn't know exactly what a homosexual was, except that they were very, very bad and disgusting men who did terrible things to children—the kind of people your parents always told you not to accept candy from.

As I grew into adolescence, I still wasn't exactly sure what a homosexual was, never having actually met one, but I knew that the most horrible thing you could call someone was a "faggot." In summer camp, there was always at least one boy who got tagged with that label. It was usually someone who couldn't throw a ball and always struck out at baseball—a total wimp, despised by the other boys and shunned by the girls. One summer, I was that boy, and while I didn't really think of being a faggot in terms of wanting to have sex with other boys, I knew there was some truth in what they were calling me. Would I, I wondered, grow up to be one of those terrible men?

When I finally met someone I knew was a homosexual, I was so relieved. Bob was a smart, handsome, and very confident college student who lived down the block. He didn't lurk behind shrubs, and he never once offered me candy. He did, however, help dispel all the myths I had grown up with about homosexuals and homosexuality. He was the first person to explain to me that a homosexual is simply a man or woman whose feelings of sexual attraction are for someone of the same sex. One man could meet and fall in love with another man, my new friend explained, and one woman could fall in love with another woman. So simple, but to me it was a revolutionary idea and it changed my life.

■ What is a lesbian?

A lesbian is a homosexual woman. The word derives from the Greek island of Lesbos, where Sappho, a teacher known for her poetry celebrating love between women, established a school for young women in the sixth century B.C. Over time, the word *lesbian*, which once simply meant someone who lived on Lesbos, came to mean a woman who, like Sappho and her followers, loved other women.

■ What is a gay person?

Gay is a synonym for *homosexual*. Since the late 1960s, the word *gay* has been publicly adopted by homosexual men and women as a positive alternative to the clinical-sounding *homosexual*. *Gay* was used as slang in place of *homosexual* as far back as the 1920s, almost exclusively within the homosexual subculture. For example, when Lisa Ben published a newsletter for lesbians called *Vice Versa* back in 1947, she gave it the tag line, "America's Gayest Magazine." Other homosexual people knew Lisa didn't mean that her magazine was simply full of fun. When Lisa spoke about herself or other lesbians, she used the phrase *gay gal*. And she described places in Los Angeles where she and her friends were welcome as being popular with a *gay crowd*.

Not all homosexual people like the word *gay*; some prefer the word *homosexual* to *gay*. And since *gay* has come to be used primarily in association with male homosexuals, many, if not most, homosexual women prefer to be called *lesbians*. Among some gay and lesbian people, the word *queer* has become popular in place of *gay* or *lesbian*. (For more on the word *queer*, see "Why do some gay people *want* to be called 'queer'?" later in this chapter.)

▪ What is a bisexual?

A bisexual person has significant feelings of sexual attraction for both men and women. These feelings may be stronger for the same sex or the opposite sex. That simply depends on the individual.

▪ Aren't bisexuals people who are afraid to admit they're gay?

Some gay and lesbian people, as they deal with accepting their feelings, may first assert that they are bisexual. That's what I did. In my last year of high school I confided to a close male friend—who I thought might be gay—that I was bisexual. By this time I already knew I was gay because I was profoundly in love with a male college student who lived next door, and I didn't have the slightest feelings of physical attraction to women. But somehow, *bisexual* didn't sound nearly as bad as *gay*. If I said I was bisexual, I rationalized, at least I was half straight. I could put one foot in the gay world and keep the other safely in the straight world—in word, if not in deed. I imagined that people would have an easier time accepting me if they thought I went both ways. But within a couple of years, when I felt more comfortable about being gay, I gave up claiming that I was bisexual.

Unfortunately, because plenty of gay and lesbian people call themselves bisexual on the way to accepting their homosexual orientation, many people have the misconception that *all* men and women who say they are bisexual are homosexuals who are afraid to admit the truth about themselves. This is simply a misconception. There are many people who have feelings of sexual attraction for both men and women.

▪ What is the Kinsey Scale?

Alfred Kinsey, whose landmark studies in the 1940s and 1950s on male and female sexuality first revealed the rich variety of human sexual expression, developed a seven-point rating scale to represent human sexual attraction. The Kinsey Scale has a range of zero to six. The zero category includes all people who are exclusively heterosexual and report no homosexual experience or attraction. Category six includes those who are exclusively homosexual in experience and attraction. Everyone else falls somewhere in between.

▪ How do you know if you're gay or lesbian?

The key to knowing whether you're heterosexual, homosexual, or bisexual is to pay attention to your feelings of attraction. The challenge for many gay, lesbian, and bisexual people is being honest with themselves about what they're feeling because society is, in general, so unaccepting of them.

Cindy, a lesbian who is now in her thirties, knew she was a lesbian by the time she was in her early teens. In college she began telling her friends that she was a lesbian and found it challenging to explain how she knew she was gay. Shortly after Cindy told her close friend Paul that she was a lesbian, she went with him to see a modern dance performance. At the time, both were juniors at a large university in the northeast. During intermission, Paul asked Cindy how she knew she was a lesbian. "It was such a simple question, but the simple ones are always the toughest to answer. I was still new at talking with straight friends about being a lesbian, so it's not like I had a standard answer. At first I thought I would ask Paul how he knew he was straight, but I didn't want to sound defensive. So I asked him how he felt when he saw one of the young women dancers on stage. He told me that, depending on which of the dancers, he might feel breathless or a tingling sensation or overwhelmed with desire. And I told him that that was just about how I felt when one of the women dancers I liked was on stage, although it takes a lot more for me to be consumed with desire than it does for Paul. But basically, I got the point across that the experience of being attracted to someone—a woman—was no different for me."

■ Can you be a gay man or a lesbian without ever having a homosexual experience or relationship?

Sexual orientation—homosexual, heterosexual, or bisexual—has everything to do with feelings of attraction and nothing to do with actual sexual experience. As you grow through childhood, you become aware of your sexual feelings. That awareness, whether it's attraction to the same sex, the opposite sex, or both sexes, does not require actual sexual experience. If you think back to your own early awareness of sexual feelings, more likely than not, you knew whether you were attracted to members of the same sex, the opposite sex, or both long before becoming sexually active.

■ Can you have homosexual feelings and not be a homosexual?
■ Can you have heterosexual feelings and not be a heterosexual?

Human sexuality is profoundly complex and not easily compartmentalized into rigid categories (as exemplified by the Kinsey Scale). So it should surprise no one that it's perfectly normal for a homosexual person to have feelings of attraction for someone of the opposite sex, just as it's perfectly normal for a heterosexual person to have feelings of attraction for someone of the same sex.

However, even though these feelings are something almost all people experience at one time or another in their lives, they can still be very confusing. The first time I had an erotic dream about a woman, I was probably nineteen or twenty. I woke up in the morning stunned, wondering how I could possibly have had such a dream after finally accepting my homosexuality. Could I have made a mistake? Was I really heterosexual? I quickly realized that one heterosexual erotic dream was just that, one heterosexual erotic dream—nothing to get upset about. My feelings for men hadn't changed, and beyond the dream I had no feelings of sexual attraction for women. After talking with friends, I discovered that I wasn't the only homosexual man who had had a heterosexual erotic dream, and some of my heterosexual friends acknowledged having had homosexual erotic dreams.

- **If you've had a homosexual experience, does that make you gay or lesbian?**
- **If you've had a heterosexual experience, does that make you heterosexual?**

Plenty of heterosexual people have had homosexual experiences, and plenty of homosexual people have had heterosexual experiences. These experiences have not changed anyone's basic sexual orientation, although they may have broadened a few horizons.

- **Don't heterosexual people who are in same-sex environments engage in homosexual behavior?**
- **Does this make them homosexuals?**

It's not uncommon for heterosexuals in restricted same-sex environments, like prisons, to engage in homosexual behavior. Their sexual orientation remains the same; they are still heterosexual and given the opportunity would choose an opposite-sex partner.

■ How many gay and lesbian people are there?

The commonly accepted figure is that one in ten people is gay or lesbian, based on Alfred Kinsey's landmark studies from the 1940s and 1950s. No definitive study has been conducted since then to confirm or refute these findings. While I suspect that the 10 percent figure is high, there are nonetheless millions of gay and lesbian Americans.

■ Have there always been gay and lesbian people?

There is every reason to believe that there have always been some people who have had feelings of attraction for those of the same sex and some people who have had physical relations with those of the same sex. At least we know it's been going on for thousands of years, as is evident from historical writings and scenes depicted in ancient art.

■ Why are there so many more gay people today than there were years ago?

This is a question my grandmother asked me. She told me that back in the 1940s, she remembers seeing one man on the subway platform in her Brooklyn neighborhood who "held his cigarette a certain way, wore a little makeup, and dressed impeccably." Because of his manner and clothing, she just assumed that he was a homosexual based on the stereotype she had grown up with. "Now you see gay people on television, read about them in the newspaper, and they have parades. Where did they all come from?"

Gay and lesbian people have always been there, but because most gay men and women look and act just like most heterosexual people, there was no way for my grandmother to know that there were lots of gay and lesbian people on the subway platform with her. The difference today is that many gay and lesbian people have publicly acknowledged to their friends, family, and colleagues that they're gay and some speak out publicly about their lives and the civil rights of gay and lesbian people.

■ How do you become a homosexual?

No one *becomes* a homosexual any more than a man or woman *becomes* a heterosexual. Feelings of attraction for one sex or the other are something we become aware of as we grow up. Where exactly these feelings come from and why some of us have strong heterosexual feelings while others have strong homosexual feelings remains a mystery.

■ Is it a choice? Why did you choose to be gay?

Just as heterosexual people don't choose their feelings of sexual attraction, gay and lesbian people don't choose theirs. All of us become aware of our feelings of sexual attraction as we grow, whether those feelings are for someone of the same sex, the opposite sex, or both sexes. For gay and lesbian people, the only real choice is between suppressing these feelings of same-sex attraction—and pretending to be asexual or hetero-sexual—and living the full emotional and physical life of a gay man or lesbian.

I like what one of my friends says whenever he's asked this question or hears someone voice the opinion that gay people make a conscious choice to be gay: "Why would I choose to be something that horrifies my parents, that could ruin my ca-reer, that my religion condemns, and that could cost me my life if I dared to walk down the street holding hands with my boyfriend?"

Although most people who live a gay or lesbian life do not have a true choice between a homosexual life or a heterosexual life, there are men and women who have feelings of sexual attraction to both sexes and therefore have the option of choosing a same-sex partner over an opposite-sex partner. One woman, who was once married to a man, explained to me that after her divorce, the first person she fell in love with happened to be a woman. "If I had fallen in love with a man first, I would have been in a heterosexual relationship instead." I hasten to add that this is not the experience of the vast majority of people who live a gay or lesbian life.

■ Are you born gay?

This debate dates back to the late 1800s, when Magnus Hirschfeld, founder of the first gay rights movement in Germany, stated his belief that homosexuality had biological origins. Now, after a few generations of accepting the psychiatric model for the origins of homosexuality, scientists are once again focusing on the biological/genetic origins of human sexuality. Though no studies have yet concluded unequivocally that sexual orientation is biologically and/or genetically based, the evidence points in that direction.

According to Chandler Burr, a journalist who is writing a book on the subject of biology and homosexuality, "The evidence, although preliminary, strongly indicates a genetic and biological basis for all sexual orientation. We see this in the work of scientists Michael Bailey and Richard Pillard, who have done studies on twins and gay and lesbian siblings. For example, they found that with identical twins, where one twin is gay, the other twin has an approximately 50 percent chance of being gay. In fraternal twins [separate eggs], if one sibling is gay, there is a 16 percent chance the other sibling will be gay. And in non-genetically related adopted brothers and sisters, where one sibling is gay or lesbian, there is a 9 percent chance that the other sibling will be homosexual, which is approximately the normal statistical incidence in the general population. These results, which indicate that sexual orientation is governed primarily by genetics, have been confirmed dramatically in other laboratories in the United States."

Chandler adds that there are other factors that contribute to sexual orientation, "which may be either biological factors— other than genetics—or 'environmental factors.'" Environmental factors, he explains, "is a term that has recently gone through a major metamorphosis in meaning. It once meant large, discrete, identifiable experiences, such as coming in contact with a gay person as a child. We now understand the 'environment' to be quite simply any and all sensory stimulation, which all people receive by virtue of being alive and living in society."

Chandler concludes, "Sexual orientation's biological component is effectively determined at birth. And we know conclusively that sexual orientation is neither changeable nor a matter of choice."

I also like what "Dear Abby," the internationally respected purveyor of commonsense advice, has to say on this subject: "I've always known that there was nothing wrong with gay and lesbian people, that this is a natural way of life for them. Nobody molested them, nobody talked them into anything. They were simply born that way. It's in the genes, and I don't think environment has a heck of a lot to do with it."

■ Is homosexuality a mental illness?

No. In response to convincing evidence, and plenty of lobbying on the part of prominent psychiatrists as well as gay rights activists, the American Psychiatric Association Board of Trustees voted in December 1973 to remove homosexuality from the *Diagnostic and Statistical Manual* as a mental illness. The American Psychological Association followed suit a little more than a year later.

It was in the mid-1950s that psychologist Dr. Evelyn Hooker first demonstrated in a landmark study that homosexual men and heterosexual men were no different psychologically. In other words, gay men were on average just as sane as their heterosexual counterparts.

■ Aren't there psychiatrists and psychologists who say they can "cure" homosexuality?

Despite the official positions of both the American Psychiatric and the American Psychological associations, there are still psychiatrists, psychoanalysts, and psychologists who claim that homosexuality is a "curable" mental illness. Others, who don't go so far as to suggest a cure for same-sex attraction, claim that they have achieved "a diminishment of homosexual feelings" among their homosexual patients, enabling them to enter heterosexual marriages and have children. But no matter what anyone claims, you cannot change a person's sexual orientation. In other words, you cannot eliminate a person's feelings of attraction for the same sex any more than you can eliminate a person's feelings of attraction for the opposite sex.

"Dear Abby" once again offers my favorite comment regarding mental health professionals who try to change homosexuals into heterosexuals: "Any therapist who would take a gay person and try to change him or her should be in jail. What the psychiatrist should do is to make the patient more comfortable with what he or she *is*—to be himself or herself."

■ What are some of the ways mental health experts and doctors have tried to "cure" homosexuals?

In the past, some mental health professionals who believed homosexual people were mentally ill or physically sick tried to "cure" gay men and lesbians using a variety of techniques, including electroshock therapy, brain surgery, hormone injections, and castration. Other methods included aversion therapy, in which, for example, male homosexuals were shown erotic pictures of men at the same time an electric shock was applied to their genitals or they were induced to vomit.

▪ Can you be seduced into being gay?

Whenever I'm asked this question I can't help but picture a heavyset, middle-aged, balding man dressed in a trench coat hiding in the bushes trying to lure young boys with candy. Despite this and other false stereotypes of how boys and girls are allegedly lured into a homosexual life, it is simply not true. A heterosexual person can't be seduced into being a gay man or lesbian any more than you can seduce a gay man or lesbian into being a heterosexual.

▪ Do gay men and lesbians recruit people to become gay?

No, gay men and lesbians do not recruit people to become gay. Can you imagine how gay and lesbian life might be advertised to potential recruits? "You, too, can be a member of a despised minority. Join us and your parents will reject you, your boss will fire you, and absolute strangers will call you names or hit you over the head with a baseball bat for holding hands with your boyfriend or girlfriend in public."

At best, gay and lesbian people can serve as positive role models for those who are struggling with their gay and lesbian identities. They can show by example that you can be homosexual and lead a full and happy life—at least as happy as anyone else's. But despite what some people may claim, gay and lesbian people do not recruit heterosexual children or adults.

▪ Are gay and lesbian people more likely to molest children?

The most likely person to molest children is a heterosexual male. His most likely victim is a female child. For example, a study conducted by Children's Hospital in Denver, Colorado, found that between July 1, 1991, and June 30, 1992, only one of 387 cases of suspected child molestation involved a gay perpetrator. Overwhelmingly, the study found that boys and girls alike said they were abused by heterosexual male family members, including fathers, stepfathers, grandfathers, and uncles. (According to Frank Bruni, a journalist who has written extensively about child molestation, "Men who molest prepubescent boys are most often—by a wide margin—heterosexual in any adult sexual involvements they may have." Frank has co-authored the forthcoming book *A Gospel of Shame: Children, Sexual Abuse, and the Catholic Church*, to be published by Viking Penguin in 1993.) But no matter how many studies are done and how many statistics are quoted, there are people who continue to promote the lie that gay or lesbian is synonymous with child molester.

▪ Do parents raise a homosexual child?

▪ Aren't gay people the result of domineering mothers and passive fathers?

You can't "raise" a homosexual child. This misconception is unfortunately supported by Sigmund Freud's flawed and long since outdated theory that a homosexual male child is the result of a strong mother and a passive, indifferent, or hostile father. Among the many flaws in Freud's theory is its failure to explain the countless examples of heterosexual sons raised by strong mothers and passive fathers and of gay sons raised by strong fathers and passive mothers. Freud also fails to explain what combination of parental personality traits lead to a lesbian daughter.

■ Is a gay person someone who was sexually abused?

There is no evidence to suggest that sexual abuse has an impact on whether a child has a heterosexual or homosexual orientation.

■ Do women become lesbians because they've had bad experiences with men?

■ Do men become gay because they've had bad experiences with women?

If all the women who had bad experiences with men became lesbians, there would be many more lesbians than heterosexual women. The fact is, bad experiences with men do not "make" heterosexual women lesbians. And bad experiences with women do not "make" heterosexual men gay. The same goes for gay and lesbian people. If they have bad experiences with people of the same sex, this does not "make" them heterosexual.

■ Are people gay because they haven't met the right man or woman?

No. How many heterosexual men and women have embarked on the challenge of "turning" a gay man or lesbian "straight," thinking that they are the "right man" or "right woman" to do the job? Before you try, you should know that a heterosexual woman cannot make a gay man heterosexual any more than a lesbian can make a heterosexual woman a lesbian. And a heterosexual man cannot turn a lesbian into a heterosexual any more than a gay man can make a heterosexual man a homosexual.

- ### Why would you want to be a lesbian when you're already oppressed as a woman?
- ### Why in a time of AIDS would you want to be a gay man?

Whether or not a lesbian or gay man *wants* to have feelings of attraction for the same sex, that's how she or he feels. And no matter how difficult the circumstances—whether sexism, the threat of AIDS, antigay violence, job discrimination, or rejection by family—these feelings of same-sex attraction will not change.

- ### Can't gay people be heterosexuals if they want to be?

No, but plenty try. The condemnation of homosexuality in our society is so great that many, if not most, gay and lesbian people *pretend* to be heterosexual, at least for part of their lives. Many lead heterosexual lives, complete with opposite-sex spouses and children. Some pretend for a lifetime, never acting on their homosexual feelings, perhaps never sharing with anyone their true feelings, taking their secret to the grave. Others find ways to accommodate their same-sex feelings through clandestine relationships and affairs. Others manage to stay married for years but ultimately divorce and seek same-sex relationships.

- ### Are gay people normal?

If normal means "in the majority," then gay and lesbian people aren't normal. But if we accept this point, then we also have to say that left-handed people are not normal, yet today we accept this physical variation as completely normal. Like left-handedness, being gay doesn't diminish anyone's humanity, his or her normal wish to love, be loved, contribute to society, and prosper.

▪ Isn't homosexuality unnatural?

Gay and lesbian people who are comfortable with their sexuality will tell you that their experience of being with someone of the same sex feels perfectly natural, whereas being with someone of the opposite sex feels unnatural. But often the underlying assumption of those who argue that homosexuality is unnatural is that penile-vaginal intercourse is the only natural way to be sexually active, and obviously a gay male couple or a lesbian couple can't have penile-vaginal intercourse.

Ann Northrop, an educator on homosexuality and AIDS, has been invited to speak to high school classes across the New York area and is often asked this question by students about whether or not homosexuality is normal. According to Ann, "I try to expand their definition of sex and ask them whether penile-vaginal intercourse is really the only way to have sex. I tell students that national surveys show that oral sex is most people's favorite form of sexual expression. But there are people who are fixated on the idea that naturalness is male-female vaginal intercourse and anything else is unnatural. That can be a tough thing to argue. Frankly, I've had a sixteen-year relationship with a woman that's monogamous and pretty happy compared to most I've seen. So I'm not too inclined to concede that I'm unnatural."

Ann, who is a Vassar-educated former CBS News producer and onetime Boston debutante, said the students may also argue that if the sexual act doesn't involve the possibility of procreation, then it isn't natural. "Then I ask them if couples who are infertile are not supposed to have sex."

- # Are humans the only animals that engage in homosexual behavior?

Scientists have observed consistent homosexual behavior in the animal kingdom in many different species ranging from the mountain ram to sea gulls to gorillas. No one has yet suggested that this is the result of a passive father and a domineering mother.

- # Is homosexuality nature's way of controlling the population?

If that was nature's purpose, she hasn't succeeded, primarily because many, if not most, gay and lesbian people—even to this day—hide their sexual feelings, enter heterosexual marriages, and have children. Besides which, a growing number of gay and lesbian individuals and couples are choosing to have children.

- # How can you tell who is a lesbian?
- # How can you tell who is a gay man?
- # Why are gay men effeminate and lesbians masculine?

For the most part, you can't tell who is gay or lesbian from appearances, unless the man or woman in question is wearing a button, a symbol, or a style of clothing that explicitly identifies him or her as gay or lesbian.

At one time we thought that gay and lesbian people were all easily identifiable by well-established stereotypical mannerisms, affectations, dress, and so on. All lesbians were thought to be masculine, and all gay men were thought to be effeminate. In fact, many effeminate men—not all—are gay, and many masculine women—not all—are lesbians. But by and large, gay and lesbian people, like all people, come in all shapes and sizes, colors, ages, as well as degrees of masculinity and femininity.

▪ Why do gay men lisp? Is it an affectation?

Some gay men lisp, as do some heterosexual men. A lisp is a type of speech defect—not an affectation—in which *s* is pronounced like *th*. For some reason it has been associated with the gay male stereotype.

Richard, who was tortured in grade school by other students because of his lisp, worked with a speech therapist for years to get rid of it. "It's ridiculous to suggest that anyone would intentionally choose to do something that would be the source of so much misery. The other kids called me a faggot, and I'm not even gay."

Do more gay men than heterosexual men lisp? That's one of those human mysteries that remains to be answered.

▪ Among gay men, is it more valued to be masculine or to be feminine?

Within American culture, masculinity in men is, in general, highly valued. Gay men are raised in the same culture as everyone else, so it should come as no surprise that masculinity is highly valued by many, if not most, gay men.

▪ Among lesbians, is it more valued to be feminine or masculine?

The young woman who suggested I include this question said that both masculinity and femininity among lesbians is valued. Masculinity, or traits that are typically associated with masculine behavior, such as aggressiveness and self-confidence, is valued by women in general, she said. And femininity, or physically feminine traits, is valued by many lesbians because it allows them to fit comfortably into society.

Ann Northrop thinks this question oversimplifies the issues. "What is feminine? What is masculine? My aim is to redefine those things. If we had a broader definition of what a man was and what masculinity was we would not be disturbed by people who are different from one narrow little stereotype.

"I'm not someone who sits around and worries about defining myself as feminine or masculine. Whoever I am is what a woman is, and it doesn't have to fit into categories of femininity and masculinity. Now, everybody is different. We are an enormously large population. You name it, we've got it. There are old bull dykes who wear pants and a vest and smoke cigars. And there are ballerinas, stewardesses, and secretaries who are lesbian as well. There is a whole spectrum of people in all communities, and the problem is that instead of recognizing our diversity, we assume we are the standard, and then we point at other people and try to narrow them and stereotype them. That's inappropriate."

▪ Why don't lesbians wear makeup? Why don't they shave?

Some lesbians wear makeup, some don't, and for all kinds of reasons. Jane said she doesn't wear makeup because "It runs on my face. I can't be bothered." Katharine wears makeup because "I look so much better." Another woman added that among some women "there is certainly the attitude that painting oneself is something you do to seduce men by some kind of game playing, so for lesbians that's irrelevant." These same points also apply to the shaving question. I should also add that there are plenty of heterosexual women who don't wear makeup and/or don't shave.

- ## Why are lesbians ugly?

Most lesbians, like most men and women, do not fit the standard for beauty in our culture. However, some lesbians are very attractive, and some are not.

- ## Why do lesbians "have a thing" for cats?

Some lesbians love cats. Some lesbians hate cats. No scientific survey has ever been conducted to establish whether or not lesbians own more cats per capita than any other group of people. This sounds like an ideal topic of market research for the people who sell cat food and related products.

- ## Why do gay men have better taste and fashion sense than straight men?

Some gay men do indeed have better taste and fashion sense than many straight men. But there are also gay men who have no taste and no fashion sense and some heterosexual men who have great taste and fashion sense.

- ## Is there a gay and lesbian culture?

I thought I'd offer an explanation of gay culture given to me by the late Chuck Rowland, one of the original founders of the Mattachine Society, a gay organization started in Los Angeles in 1950. Chuck was one of the first people to argue that there was a gay and lesbian culture. When I interviewed him in 1989, he told me that he had an especially hard time in the 1950s explaining to other gay people what he meant by gay culture. "People would say, 'Gay culture? What do you mean? Do you actually think we're more cultured than anybody else?' I would explain that I was using 'culture' in the sociological sense, as a body of language, feelings, thinking, experiences that we share in common. As we speak of a Mexican culture. As we speak of an American Indian culture.

"We had to say that gay culture was an emergent culture. For example, as gay people, we used certain language, certain words. The word *gay* itself is a marvelous example of what I mean by gay culture. You'll get a lot of argument about this. But I know that *gay* was being used back in the thirties, and we didn't mean 'merry' or 'festive.' We meant 'homosexual.' This does not constitute a language in the sense that English is a language and French is a language, but it's more comparable to Yiddish culture. A lot of people, Jews and non-Jews, use Yiddish words like *schlepp, meshuga*, a dozen others. This separates them culturally from my mother, for example, who would never have heard of such words. A lot of people still don't agree with the gay culture issue. But you see the term *gay culture* all the time now."

In the decades since Chuck Rowland first made his case for the existence of gay culture, a very significant body of work that we would normally associate with the cultural life of a community has been created primarily for gay and lesbian people by gay and lesbian writers, artists, photographers, playwrights, choreographers, filmmakers, and so forth.

■ Why do some gay people want to be called "queer"?

Plenty of gay and lesbian people are puzzled by this one as well. Some gay and lesbian people have chosen the word *queer* because they feel it is more inclusive than gay and lesbian. And they feel that by "reclaiming" a word that has been used by those who hate gay people, they have stripped it of its original hurtful intent and transformed it into something positive.

According to one woman in her mid-twenties, "While some people find this word offensive, many of us find it liberating be-

cause it is a word that embraces us all. We use it as a word of
pride, of inclusion, and of community. The word reflects the
painful reality that regardless of how we identify ourselves, we
are all outside the heterosexual majority, and we all suffer prejudice, discrimination, hatred, and ignorance from the majority
population."

■ Why do some gay and lesbian people call themselves "fags" and "dykes"?

Like other minority groups, some gay and lesbian people
playfully use words that are used by the larger population to
put them down. Some say it's a way of taking the sting out of
these words.

Warning: You can only use these words playfully if you
yourself are gay or lesbian. And bear in mind that plenty of gay
and lesbian people do not like the words *fag* or *dyke* no matter
the sexual orientation of the person using them.

■ What does "breeders" mean?

A friend of mine was standing at a counter at an ice cream
shop on Castro Street, the main commercial street of San Francisco's predominantly gay and lesbian neighborhood. While he
was ordering ice cream for himself and his adopted daughter, a
gay man standing beside him at the counter turned to him and
said with a sneer, "breeder." This is a term—not exactly affectionate—that some gay people use against heterosexuals, that
is, people who have children—breeders. Unfortunately, the man
who called my friend a breeder mistakenly assumed that he was
heterosexual. In fact, he's a gay man in a long-term relationship
raising a daughter. This just goes to show that gay people can
also make stereotyped assumptions and say hateful things.

- ## What do I do if a gay person makes a pass at me?

If you're not interested, you say, "No thank you." If you *are* interested, you can make your interest known in a variety of ways. (See chapter 5, "Dating.")

- ## What is the "gay lifestyle"?

Not long ago, just after moving back to New York, a woman friend of mine told me that she was worried I'd go out and lead a wild "gay lifestyle." I don't know how many times I've said there is no such thing as a "gay lifestyle," wild or otherwise, but I knew exactly what my friend was talking about. What she feared I would do was go out dancing all night at gay clubs, drink too much, take drugs, probably take my shirt off when things got too hot, and maybe even have unsafe sex in the balcony overlooking the dance floor.

After watching countless news reports and occasional documentaries over the years about gay people—gay men mostly—the popular image of gay life that has been seared into the minds of most Americans is the urban, single nightlife led by some gay men—and plenty of straight people as well—during the 1970s.

As hard as it might be to believe, there is no such thing as a "gay lifestyle," just as there is no such thing as a heterosexual lifestyle. Gay and lesbian people, like heterosexual people, live in a variety of ways, from poor to middle-class to nouveau riche, from urban to rural.

- ## Don't gay people make more money?

Although accurate statistics are hard to come by, gay people, on average, are as diverse in the amount of money they earn as are heterosexual people. However, those gay and lesbian people who do not have children to support, like those heterosexual people who do not have children to support, have higher disposable incomes.

When it comes to gay and lesbian couples, there is a notable difference in combined income in comparison to heterosexual couples, whether or not there are children to support. Gay male couples are likely to have higher combined incomes than heterosexual couples because two men are likely to earn more money than a man and a woman; on average, women are paid less than men. By contrast, lesbian couples, on average, have lower combined incomes than heterosexual couples because two women are likely to earn less money than a man and a woman.

▪ Do gay men hate women?
▪ Do lesbians hate men?

In general, no. But some gay men do hate women, just as some heterosexual men hate women. And some gay men hate men, despite the fact they have sexual feelings for men. And some lesbians hate men, just as some heterosexual women hate men. And some lesbians hate women, despite the fact they have sexual feelings for women. The bottom line is, everyone is capable of hating, no matter what his or her sexual orientation or gender.

▪ Do gay men and lesbians hate straight people?

In general, no. But some gay and lesbian people have hostile feelings toward heterosexual people. This should come as no surprise, given some of the terrible things gay and lesbian people have experienced at the hands of heterosexual people. (See chapter 12, "Discrimination.")

2

SELF-DISCOVERY—GROWING UP

- **When do you first become aware of your homosexual feelings?**
- **Is there any difference between men and women with regard to when they become aware of their homosexual feelings?**

People who have feelings of attraction for the same sex most often become aware of these feelings at the same time all people become aware of their feelings of attraction, whether that's from earliest conscious memory or during pre-adolescence or adolescence, or later. But there are differences. For heterosexual people these feelings are reinforced—by family, society, culture, religion—from the earliest age. For example, how many times have you heard loving relatives ask a young child if he has a girlfriend or she has a boyfriend? Even if it's asked in the most playful way, this question reinforces that boys have girlfriends and girls have boyfriends.

For a gay or lesbian child growing up, the experience is very different. Even before they're fully aware of their feelings of attraction or the implications of these feelings, gay and lesbian kids know that what they're feeling isn't how things are supposed to be. That was Deborah's experience: "Growing up was quite traumatic for me because I really thought that I was a little boy trapped inside a little girl's body. I was supposed to be sweet and docile, but I was a jock. I wanted to grab the world by the balls! It just didn't make any sense to me. And I had sexual feelings very, very early, but boys were not an interest. When the other little girls were starting to get crushes on boys and were talking about weddings, I always knew I wanted to marry a girl—always, always, always. When I was seven, I remember telling my parents that I was not going to marry a man and all the reasons why. By the time I was ten, I explained to them that I was in love with this little girl. My dad told me that it was just a phase, that I was going to outgrow it.

"I didn't know there was such a thing as lesbianism, women with women, so I just assumed that I would have to be a male if I wanted to be with women. It was very confusing. It was when I read *The Children's Hour* in seventh grade that I learned about women with women. I was doing a scene with this woman I had a serious crush on, and she got to the part where she explained how she really felt for her female co-worker. It hit me like a ton of bricks. 'That's what this is!'"

Beyond the confusion of not understanding why you're different from other kids, and the confusion of having a parent tell you that you'll "outgrow it," for example, gay and lesbian kids often get daily negative reinforcement of what they're feeling, whether that's religious condemnation of homosexuality, kids using the words *fag* and *dyke* or *lezzie* at school, or jokes about gay people in the movies. Because of this negative reinforcement, most gay and lesbian people hide their sexual orientation, pretend to be straight, and wait at least until after high school to deal with their sexual orientation and act on their feelings. Some gay and lesbian people may repress their feelings of sexual attraction for years and may lead heterosexual lives that include marriage, children, and grandchildren without ever telling another soul about their homosexuality.

Some gay people—and generally I hear this from women, rarely from men—don't become fully aware of their feelings of sexual attraction until they reach their thirties, forties, or later. That was Mary Elizabeth's experience: "When I was still in my teens, Mother used to tell me not to wear my hair short or wear tailored clothing. I never understood what she was talking about. It took me until I was nearly forty-five, married, with two grown kids to figure out what she was getting at. Mother was afraid that if I looked and dressed like a lesbian that I'd become one. Mother knew what was up long before I did! I sure as hell wish she'd said something to me before she died, because it took me forever to realize what she knew all along. I know some people won't believe this, but I really didn't know I had these feelings until I fell in love with Eileen. And she was married, too!"

- **Do people who are gay or lesbian feel bad about it?**

- **Do they always feel this way?**

- **Why are gay and lesbian people so angry?**

Feel bad? When I was a teenager, I thought my life was over. How could I be something that was considered so disgusting, so loathsome, so awful? How could I be what people called a homo, a queer, a pansy, a sissy, a child molester, a fag, for God's sake? (At the time I grew up, there were virtually no positive gay images or role models.) What I didn't know until later was that feeling bad about my feelings of attraction to men was a perfectly normal reaction to what I had learned from the world around me about homosexuals and the kinds of lives they were "sentenced to lead."

The statistics on suicide sadly confirm how unhappy many people are about being gay or lesbian—especially while they're first dealing with their feelings of attraction for the same sex. A 1988 study commissioned by the U.S. Department of Health and Human Services found gay adolescents commit suicide at two to three times the rate of heterosexuals, and some studies say that 40 percent of all homosexuals make attempts on their lives when they're young.

Those gay and lesbian people who survive their adolescence and go on to accept their sexual orientation find that self-hate, the desire to die—all those bad feelings—change and often become feelings of rage and anger. People feel angry about being lied to by religious leaders, judged by their parents, misled by psychiatrists, and condemned by society in general. They're angry at their lost adolescence, or in the case of people who don't come to accept their sexuality until later in life, they're angry about having "wasted" their lives living a lie. In time, for most gay and lesbian people, this anger recedes—although it doesn't necessarily go away.

Not every gay or lesbian person goes through the experience of feeling bad about him or herself, although *not* feeling bad is by far the exception. Dan knew exactly what he was from the second grade and also knew that there was nothing wrong: "I don't know how I knew I was okay and the world was wrong, but I just knew it. In elementary school I liked other boys, and that felt right to me, so from then on I never paid attention to the name-calling. And besides that, my uncle is gay and everyone loves him, so being gay was never a big deal in my family. Sure, my parents weren't thrilled when I told them, but that was mostly because they worried about discrimination and AIDS."

■ How do gay people accept that they are gay or lesbian?

Many, if not most, gay and lesbian people have difficulty accepting their feelings because accepting these feelings of same-sex attraction means unlearning what are likely to be deeply held negative beliefs about homosexuals and homosexuality.

People learn to accept themselves through a variety of means. They may do their own personal research, reading everything they can find on the subject of homosexuality, or they may be lucky enough to find role models. They may also join support groups for gay and lesbian people or enter therapy.

Not everyone who is gay or lesbian does accept it. Some people struggle to repress what they're feeling, denying even to themselves what they know in their hearts and minds. Some people search for a "cure" through therapy, religion, or an organization that promises to show "the way out of the homosexual lifestyle." There is, of course, no cure for homosexuality, because you can no more cure a man's or woman's feelings of same-sex attraction than you can cure a man's or woman's feelings of opposite-sex attraction.

■ Do gay people like being gay or lesbian?

This question reminds me of a related question that I've often been asked: If you could take a pill and become a heterosexual, would you? This question presumes that life would be better as a heterosexual. When I was seventeen, I would have said yes in a second. I didn't like being gay. I wanted to be "normal." I wanted to be like everyone else. I wanted to find a relationship, get married, hold hands on the street, and be able to proclaim my love for another person in public. I didn't want to be different. But by the time I was in my early twenties, I wasn't so sure I wanted to take such a pill, because my life as a gay man wasn't so bad, and I was getting used to it. Also, from what I saw, I knew there was no guarantee that life would be any better as a heterosexual person, and it could also be worse. By my mid-twenties I realized this was a ridiculous question, because there was no such pill, and by then I had already decided that there were far more terrible things in life than being gay, and I should make the most of who I was, even if that was something society didn't like. Now I wouldn't want to be any different, because I like who I am, and part of that is being gay.

I don't pretend to speak for everyone, but when Ann Landers asked her readers to write in and tell her if they were glad to be gay, she got tens of thousands of letters in response, most of them (thirty to one) from gay and lesbian people who were glad to be who they were. (Of course, there are also many gay and lesbian people who are not happy about who they are, but I imagine they were less likely to make the effort to respond to the Ann Landers column.)

I put this question to several different gay and lesbian people and they offered several different responses. Among those who like being gay, some people said they can no longer imagine being any different, that they've grown accustomed to who they are. Others feel that they're more sensitive and more insightful people because of their experience of growing up in a world where they're outsiders. Others feel lucky to have been given the opportunity to lead something other than a traditional life, in which you progress from single life, to marriage, to children, without thinking whether or not this is really something you want to do. The experience of growing up gay, many told me, led them to ask questions about many of life's assumptions—like getting married and having children—that most heterosexual people never examine.

Those who had negative feelings about being gay also offered a variety of reasons for their feelings. Some said they would have better luck finding a spouse if they were heterosexual, or that being gay has held them back in their careers, or that being gay has made it difficult, if not impossible, to have children.

- ### What's it like to be a gay or lesbian teenager?
- ### What's it like for gay and lesbian kids in high school?

I have only a handful of vivid memories of my high school years, a time when I was just beginning to come to terms with being gay. One of those memories is from a Sunday afternoon party in the spring of 1976, during my senior year at Hillcrest High School in New York City. About twenty of us were scattered around the living room of a friend's apartment. Across from where I was standing, my friend Ruth was sitting on a big easy chair, with her boyfriend on one arm of the chair and our friend Dave on the other. I was pretty sure by then that Dave was gay; we'd just started dropping hints to each other a few weeks before. (We even admitted to each other that we might be bisexual.) Everyone was listening to Ruth, who somehow worked her way onto the subject of gay people and declared, "I guess it's okay with me, but I wouldn't want one of them near me." Instantly, Dave and I locked eyes. Ruth had no idea that the man sitting next to her was gay (Dave told me he was gay after we graduated), and that the friend who picked her up every day for three years to go to school—me!—was also gay. "What would she think?" I wondered. "Would she still want to be my friend?"

I had hoped that life for gay and lesbian teenagers had improved dramatically since I graduated from high school. But that's not what I've found. Though gay and lesbian teens have many more positive role models today, and in a handful of places access to knowledgeable counselors who are trained to deal with lesbian and gay teens, not a lot has changed. Most gay and lesbian kids do everything they can to pass as straight and keep their sexual orientation a secret from their friends, family, teachers, and school counselors. Most of those who are thought to be gay or lesbian, or who come out (tell their friends that they're gay) or are found out, may be verbally or physically tormented by other students. And one third of teenage suicides involve gay and lesbian teens.

Elliott, who is finishing high school early to get away from his tormentors, never managed to pass as straight at his suburban Dallas high school. "Since the very first day, some of the kids have called me *sissy* and *fag* in the halls. They try to trip me all the time, and someone once wrote 'AIDS victim' on my locker. It's been absolute hell." Elliott hasn't had much better luck with his mother. He moved out of her house at the start of his senior year and now lives with a friend's family several blocks away. "My mom didn't want me meeting other gay people, so I'd have to sneak out. Of course, she caught me a few times, and it got real ugly. I had to get away."

There are, thankfully, exceptions. Tammy, who is now in college, found a group of supportive friends—straight and gay—on her high school volleyball team. "I always knew I was lucky," she said, "to have a group of friends when I was that young I didn't have to keep secrets from. It really helped me accept being gay. There were a couple of other lesbians on the team, and we were all out to each other and the rest of the team. I don't know, maybe it was just the right time or it was the right group of people, or maybe it's finally sinking in that there's nothing wrong with us."

▪ What do heterosexual teenagers think of their gay and lesbian peers?

Besides all the things you would expect teenagers to think and feel about their gay and lesbian peers—from easy acceptance to thoughts of physical violence—educator Ann Northrop found something I would never have expected. Ann said, "Many of these teenagers are furious at their gay or lesbian peers for hiding. They think they're liars, and cheats, and deceivers, and manipulators. But the fact is, these gay and lesbian kids are afraid—mostly of being rejected. So when you explain to teenagers what's really going on, that these gay and lesbian kids are not being criminals or betrayers, and explain how much pain and terror they're experiencing, then they say, 'Oh, I get it. I didn't want to be mean to that person for that.'

"I also tell these kids, 'It's up to you to make the first move. Do not expect your gay and lesbian friends to come to you and tell you they're gay if you have not given them a signal that it's okay to talk to you.'"

▪ What are students taught in high school about homosexuality?

▪ Isn't there a gay high school?

See chapter 16, "Education."

▪ Do gay teens take same-sex dates to the high school prom? Why, or why not?

It doesn't happen often, but it's been done. The most celebrated example involved a high school senior named Aaron Fricke, who, in 1980, took a male date to his high school senior prom in Cumberland, Rhode Island. Aaron's story is celebrated because he sued his high school for the right to take his same-sex date. Aaron later wrote a wonderful account of that story in his book *Reflections of a Rock Lobster*.

Though Aaron's story is the best known, the earliest stories I came across about high school students taking same-sex dates to proms involved two young men at a high school in Medford, Massachusetts, in 1975, and two young women at Girls High in Philadelphia, Pennsylvania, in 1976.

Teenagers who take same-sex dates to their high school proms do it for the same reason heterosexual teenagers do: because they want to go with the date of their choice. As Aaron Fricke wrote, "The simple, obvious thing would have been to go to the senior prom with a girl. But that would have been a lie—a lie to myself, to the girl, and to all the other students. What I *wanted* to do was to take a male date."

But Aaron had other reasons for taking a same-sex date, which went well beyond wanting simply to take someone of his own choosing. Like most of the students who have taken same-sex dates to high school proms, he wanted to make a statement about who he was—a gay man—and his rights as a gay person.

Before Aaron made his final decision, he carefully thought out all the implications and considered both how what he might do would benefit him and what impact it would have on the other students. Aaron wrote, "I believed that those who had themselves faced discrimination or prejudice would immediately understand what I was doing and its implications for human rights. There would be others who may never have had direct experiences with prejudice but who would recognize my right to take the date of my choice. These people may have been misled to believe that homosexuality is wrong, but they could still understand that my rights were being denied.

"At the opposite end of the spectrum were the homophobics who might react violently. But the example I set would be perfect for everyone. We would be just one more happy couple. Our happiness together would be something kids could relate to. I would be showing that my dignity and value as a human being were not affected by my sexual preference.

"I concluded that taking a guy to the prom would be a strong positive statement about the existence of gay people. Any opposition to my case (and I anticipated a good bit) would show the negative side of society—not homosexuality.

"To attend the prom with a girl would not be unenjoyable but it would be dishonest to my true feelings. Besides, most kids now knew I was gay. If I went with a female, I would probably have received more taunts than from going with a male. By going with a male I would win some respect from the more mature students, and I would keep my self-esteem."

Most gay and lesbian teenagers don't take same-sex dates to their high school proms, and for many reasons: They haven't yet come to terms with their sexual orientation or aren't yet fully aware of these feelings, so they wouldn't think of taking a same-sex date to the prom. They don't want the other students to know that they're gay or lesbian. They don't want their parents to find out that they're gay or lesbian. They don't want to be the focus of attention or can't find a date willing to be the focus of attention, which a same-sex couple inevitably will be. Or, like plenty of heterosexual kids, they simply can't find a date.

■ If you're a teenager and think you're gay or lesbian, what should you do?

If you think you're gay, lesbian, bisexual, whatever, and you haven't got anyone to talk to about your feelings, find someone you can trust—and talk. You'll feel better if you share what you're thinking with someone else. If there isn't anyone in your life you can trust—a best friend, a sibling, a school counselor—you have other options. In many major cities there are discussion groups just for gay, lesbian, and bisexual young people. You can find these groups by looking in the phone book or calling a local gay help line. You can also call or write the Hetrick-Martin Institute in New York, a private nonprofit organization that provides all kinds of services to gay and lesbian youth. You can talk to someone there, or they'll help you find someone to talk to in your city. You can also call the local chapter of Parents and Friends of Lesbians and Gays (P-FLAG). At P-FLAG you'll find an accepting mom or dad who has lots of experience with these issues and will be more than happy to talk to you. (The Hetrick-Martin Institute, in general, recommends that gay and lesbian teens *not* tell their own parents that they are gay because of the danger of being thrown out of the house and/or cut off financially.)

Hetrick-Martin Institute
401 West Street
New York, NY 10014
Tel: 212-633-8920
TTY: 212-633-8926
Parents and Friends of Lesbians and Gays (P-FLAG)
To get the telephone number of your local chapter, check your telephone book or call 1-800-4-FAMILY.

3

COMING OUT—GOING PUBLIC

▪ What does "coming out of the closet" mean?

To explain how a gay or lesbian person "comes out of the closet," you first need to know what "the closet" is. The closet is simply a metaphor used to describe the place gay and lesbian people keep their sexual orientation hidden—whether that place is between their ears, within a tightly knit group of friends, or within the larger gay and lesbian community. The truth is kept "behind the closet door."

At its most basic, "coming out of the closet" means being honest with those around you—friends, family, colleagues, and so forth—about your sexual orientation, about who you are. For example, that might mean talking about your same-sex spouse if a new colleague asks you if you're married. But coming out of the closet means different things to different people. When you ask three different gay and lesbian people to talk about their coming-out experiences, you're likely to get three entirely different stories. One will talk about coming out sexually—his or her first sexual experience. Another will talk about coming out to herself—when she first accepted the fact she was a lesbian. Still another will talk about coming out to his family—when he first told his family that he was gay.

▪ What's it like living in the closet?

"It's exhausting and frightening," said Beverly, who spent more than a dozen years in the military hiding the fact she was a lesbian. "I never knew when the ax would fall, when someone would turn me in. At any moment I knew my career could be over. So I watched everything I said, everything I did, to make sure no one would guess the truth. I tell you, it was the hardest thing I ever did in my life. I thought I was going to lose my mind."

Even if your job doesn't depend on keeping your sexual orientation hidden, staying in the closet can be hard work. You've got to live two different lives—your real life and a life that's suitable for public consumption. You have to monitor what you say and be careful of what you do, and you have to make certain your two lives never intersect. When you attend office functions, you've got to bring a date of the opposite sex, even if you've been living with your same-sex partner for twenty years. When your kids visit you and your same-sex spouse for the weekend, you have to pretend that you're roommates and make certain you've left no incriminating evidence anywhere in the house. (Kids are curious, and if there's something to be found, they'll find it.) Above all, you've got to be an expert story teller. You've got to be able to tell a convincing lie with a straight face.

When I was a teenager, I was terribly frightened that people would find out I was gay. I worked hard to keep my secret, and I made up all kinds of stories to cover my tracks. Once when I was home on vacation during my first year in college, I went out with some gay friends on a Friday night. I told my mother some story about where I was going and with whom. And I told my girlfriend from high school, who was also home from college, another story. I didn't mean to tell two different stories, but I couldn't remember what I'd told my mother. So there we were the next evening, the three of us, in the living room at my mother's house, and Eileen asked me how my Friday night party had been. Well, I couldn't remember what story I'd told my mother, but it was clear from the expression on her face that I hadn't told her I was at a party. Eileen saw the expression on my mother's face and the look of horror on my face, and there was a split second when everyone realized I'd been caught in a lie. It was in that moment that I realized I didn't have the talent—or the memory—required to keep my life a secret. I was a failure at staying in the closet. Fortunately, I have a family that accepts me as I am and a career that doesn't require me to hide.

Many people are experts at keeping their homosexuality carefully hidden and don't find it especially difficult. Tom is in his early fifties, in a relationship with a man for more than two decades, and deep in the closet to everyone but his close circle of gay male friends. As far as his colleagues know, he's a confirmed bachelor who has no life beyond his career. "I learned a long time ago how to keep my two worlds—my personal life and my professional life—entirely separate. I never socialize with people from work and never discuss anything about my personal life with my colleagues. My lover and I have separate phones at home, both of which are unlisted, so even if someone suspected I had a lover, they could never trace us through the phone company.

"I would never have gotten as far as I have in my career if it were known that I'm gay, and I'm not about to risk all I have just so I can bring my partner to company parties. It's not worth it. Years ago, when I was growing up, there was no choice. No one ever talked about coming out of the closet, because it would have been such an outrageous thing to do. Only crazy people didn't hide. You *had* to keep it hidden. Now there's a choice, but I'm happy and very comfortable with the way I live my life."

▪ Why do people stay in the closet?

Gay and lesbian people stay in the closet for three primary reasons: necessity, fear, and because they simply prefer not to discuss this part of their lives with, for example, their colleagues or families.

Those who stay in the closet because of necessity may do so because they know or suspect they'll lose their jobs or, for example, because they think their parents will stop paying their college tuition or throw them out of the house if they find out.

Fear is often a factor when people decide it's a necessity to hide their sexual orientation. People fear being rejected by their families, fear losing or compromising their careers, fear losing custody of their children, fear being thrown out of the house, fear physical violence at the hands of those who hate gay people, fear being judged, and so forth. And much of the fear is justified by the horror stories we have heard, read, and experienced personally.

▪ Why do gay people feel they have to tell anybody?
▪ Why can't they keep it to themselves?

Most gay and lesbian people keep their sexual orientation to themselves, and the price of keeping the secret can be high, whether the price is counted in the stunning number of gay and lesbian teens who kill themselves or in the high rate of alcoholism and drug abuse among gay people. There are also, of course, many gay men and women who are comfortable with and are accustomed to keeping their homosexuality hidden, and they do whatever they have to in order to conceal their sexual orientation.

Those gay and lesbian people who choose to tell their friends, family, and colleagues about their sexual orientation do so for many reasons. However, they do it primarily because they want to be themselves, because they want to be honest with those they love and trust, and because it can be difficult, exhausting, and personally destructive to pretend to be someone you're not.

Imagine for a moment what it's like to "keep it to yourself." It's Monday morning at the office, and one of your colleagues asks you what you did for the weekend. You answer, as you always do, "Nothing much," even though you spent the weekend at the hospital with your seriously ill spouse. You could have said that you spent the weekend in the hospital with a person close to you, but more questions would inevitably follow, and ultimately it would be impossible to hide the truth. So to protect your secret, you can almost never honestly respond to an innocent question or comment, whether the question is asked by a colleague, a relative, or even a cab driver. You have to monitor everything you say.

As a test, just take note during an average day how many times your personal life comes up in conversation, whether you're at a mall buying clothes or stuck on the phone with a telephone salesperson. Imagine how you would respond if you had to hide your life. If you were a gay man in a long-term relationship and a telephone salesperson called and asked for the "woman of the house," how would you answer? Would you say, "We're not interested," and hang up? Or would you say,

"I'm a man and so is my spouse, so there is no 'woman of the house.'" Or you could do what a friend of mine does who has gotten so fed up with telemarketers that instead of simply saying there's no woman in the house, he answers in his deep, resonant, unmistakably male voice, "You're talking to her."

- **Why do people choose to come out of the closet to their parents?**
- **Why do gay and lesbian people choose *not* to come out of the closet to their parents?**

People choose to tell their parents that they're gay or decide not to tell them for all the same reasons gay people generally have for coming out or not coming out. But telling parents or not telling parents is often a more emotionally profound and complex decision than is the decision to come out to friends and colleagues.

Michelle, an accountant in her late twenties who lives in Atlanta, finally told her parents she was a lesbian after thinking about doing it for nearly ten years. "At first I couldn't get past the fear they would reject me. When I was still living at home, I thought they'd throw me out of the house. Then I was afraid they'd pull me out of college. After college I was still afraid they would reject me, but that was compounded by my fear that I'd disappoint them; they had always been so proud of my accomplishments. I never liked keeping secrets from them, but I didn't find it terribly difficult as long as I wasn't dating anyone. But then I fell in love and began a serious relationship. There was so much I wanted to tell my parents, but all we wound up talking about was the weather and the cows (my parents are dairy farmers). I knew they were worried about me being alone, but if I told them I wasn't alone and that my roommate was my lover, I was afraid of destroying their lives. Finally I got up my courage to tell them. It was so hard to say the words, but it was an incredible relief to finally have it out in the open. That was several years ago now, and my parents are doing okay. It's not easy for them to talk about it, but they're making a good effort."

Steve, like many people who choose *not* to come out to their parents, doesn't see any reason why he should discuss the fact he's gay with his parents. "I'm nearly forty, and I've never discussed anything personal with them about any aspect of my life, so why would I talk about this? Besides, they live halfway across the country, so I only see them once or twice a year. Why make trouble, why burden them, when it won't accomplish anything?" Steve resents the pressure some of his friends have put on him to tell his parents the truth. "It's my choice, and it works for me. There's no law that says I have to come out to them if I don't want to. If I thought it would make my life better, I'd think about it. Some of my friends say I would have a closer relationship with my parents if I told them, but I don't want a closer relationship with them."

▪ How do gay people come out of the closet?

There are many different ways to let people know you're gay. Some people write letters to their parents or friends or do it face-to-face in conversation. Others drop hints, hoping that someone will ask a question that will give them an opportunity to answer truthfully. Still others go on television talk shows, or like the actor Dick Sargent, veteran of the popular "Bewitched" television series, choose to come out in *People* magazine. Whatever the choice, the decision to come out is likely one that a gay or lesbian person has thought about and agonized over for a very long time.

In general, coming out is not something you do just once and then forget about. For gay and lesbian people who choose to live out of the closet, coming out is something you may do almost every day. There are all kinds of chance encounters and conversations that force gay people to decide whether to answer honestly or not. For example, I sat down next to a woman on a train from New York to Washington the other day, and within minutes she asked me if I was married. I said that I wasn't. She then asked if I had a girlfriend. I said that I didn't, and she asked if I would be interested in meeting her sister. I could have just said no, and left it at that, but if I were straight, I might have been interested in meeting her sister. The truth was, because I'm gay, it would have been an inappropriate match, so I told her that I was flattered, but that I was gay and her sister probably wouldn't be interested in me. Then she asked if I would be interested in meeting her boss, who was gay, single, and about my age.

Not every gay and lesbian person has to say anything to let people know that he or she is gay. Dave and Judy, best friends and neighbors for more than ten years, told me they never have to tell anyone that they're gay. "We couldn't pass for straight in this lifetime," said Judy, "no matter how hard we tried. We're living proof that the gay stereotype came from somewhere." Dave is very slight, has delicate features, and is extremely effeminate. Judy is a self-described "big butch." She's built like a construction worker, is partial to jeans and sweatshirts, and has a very deep voice. "We're always getting harassed," said Dave, "because people can tell. Sometimes we envy people who can pass, but in a lot of ways it's easier for us. Because we can't hide, we've never had to worry about coming out. We were out before we even knew what we were."

▪ What's it like to come out of the closet?

When Gary, who grew up in a very small southwestern town, came out of the closet to his family, friends, and colleagues on a national television talk show, he felt an incredible sense of relief and renewal. "It was like being born. The burden had been lifted from my shoulders. For the first time I felt like I had a life. It was the first time I stood up and said, 'This is who I am, and I'm proud of who I am.' For someone who was always embarrassed about being gay, that wasn't easy, especially on national television. And it took me until I was thirty-five to do it. But it was important for me to do it for myself and to set an example for young people, to show them there's a better way, that you don't have to hide the way I did and waste all those years. My only regret about the whole experience was that I hadn't done it sooner. Of course, I felt bad about upsetting my parents, but it'd been on *my* shoulders since I was a kid. It was time for them to deal with it. It wasn't my problem anymore."

I can't speak for all gay and lesbian people, but most of the hundreds of gay men and lesbians I've interviewed in the past five years have told me that coming out has ultimately been a positive experience. And that group includes people who have lost their jobs or been rejected by their families and even their children. The experience may have been painful, traumatic, frightening, and overwhelming, but almost none of the people I've spoken with have said they regret living life free of the closet.

▪ When do gay and lesbian people come out of the closet?

I know a woman who told her parents that she wanted to marry another girl when she was seven years old. I don't know if you would call this coming out of the closet, but she certainly alarmed her parents. And I know a man who didn't tell another soul he was gay until he was nearly eighty-five. More typically, those gay and lesbian people who choose to come out start sharing the truth about their sexuality with friends and family from their late teens through their twenties.

▪ Why do they have to flaunt it?

My uncle once said to me, "Okay, I can understand wanting to be truthful about who you are, but why do gays have to flaunt it all the time?" When he asked that question, my uncle and I were sitting on beach chairs just a few feet away from the picnic table where my uncle's mother-in-law was playing Scrabble with my friends Peter and Eleanor, who were just a couple of months away from being married. At that moment, Peter was stroking Eleanor's back in a very tender and loving way. I called my uncle's attention to the obvious public display of affection and asked him if he considered what Peter was doing with Eleanor "flaunting." He got my point. What we generally consider normal behavior for heterosexual people— talking about a romantic interest or relationship, an affectionate peck on the cheek between husband and wife, holding hands in public, or stroking the back of your beloved—we call "flaunting" when gay and lesbian people do it.

Most gay people, like heterosexual people, have no desire to make a spectacle of themselves. They just want to be themselves in the same way that heterosexual people are. Many times I've heard lesbian and gay people say—and I've said it, too—how wonderful it would be to hold hands when walking down the street with a boyfriend, girlfriend, or spouse without having to worry that someone was going to call you names or come at you with a baseball bat.

▪ Why do gay activists urge people to come out?

Most gay and lesbian rights activists want to achieve widespread acceptance of gay and lesbian people and equal rights under the law. These two goals can't be achieved, they believe, as long as most heterosexual people continue to believe the negative stereotypes about gay and lesbian people.

And the only way these myths will be destroyed is if heterosexual people discover they already know and love someone who is gay or lesbian. But the only way they will find out they know gay men and women is for gay people to be honest, to come out of the closet. This is why gay and lesbian leaders speak about the importance of gay and lesbian visibility and the necessity of coming out of the closet.

I asked Ann Northrop this question of why gay and lesbian people should come out. Ann, who is a nationally prominent activist in addition to being an experienced educator, put personal happiness first on the list of reasons: "They'll feel so much better and be so much happier, which was my experience. The frustration is knowing people are closeted and terrified and not having a way to communicate to them how much happier they would be if they came out. Then once everyone comes out, the world will be a different place, because suddenly we'll be everywhere, and people will be forced to deal with the reality of who we are rather than the stereotypes. It's the only way the world will be transformed. We all have to be visible for the world to change. But most important, people should come out because they will be happier."

▪ What is National Coming Out Day?

National Coming Out Day, which has been celebrated every October 11 since 1988, commemorates the October 11, 1987, gay and lesbian rights march on Washington, D.C. The annual celebration is coordinated by an educational nonprofit organization called National Coming Out Day. According to the organization's executive director, "We're a visibility campaign that encourages people to tell the truth about their lives—to come out of the closet, so we can put to rest the myths that people have used against us. And we're dedicated to seeing the lesbian and gay community participate fully, openly, and equally in society. To reach that goal, we encourage groups and individuals across the country and around the world to plan events on and around National Coming Out Day that promote visibility."

National Coming Out Day is now marked by events in places all over the world, including New Zealand, India, Thailand, Great Britain, Canada, and Siberia. For example, some communities raise money to place ads in local city newspapers that list the names of people who have decided to come out of the closet. One group in Denver, Colorado, paid for five billboards that said, "Coming Out Means Telling the Truth About Your Life, a Real Family Value." Another group in Philadelphia holds its annual block party every October 11.

4

FAMILY AND CHILDREN

- ## What constitutes a gay or lesbian family?

Leslie and Joanna and their infant daughter Emily are a family. David and Edward, who just celebrated their twenty-fifth anniversary as a couple, are a family. Al, who divorced his wife because he is gay, and his two teenage sons who live with him full-time are a family. Evelyn, a retired math teacher, and three of her friends, all lesbians, who share a large home on Cape Cod are a family. These families may not meet the "Ozzie and Harriet" model of family life, but then most families don't. What these families *do* have is what all families ought to have: love, care, concern, and commitment to the health, happiness, and well-being of each family member.

- ## Are gay and lesbian people antifamily?

- ## Are gay and lesbian rights groups trying to destroy the American family?

Despite what some antigay activists have said, gay and lesbian people and gay and lesbian rights organizations do not want to destroy America's family values or the American family. Why would any group of people or any organization set as its goal the destruction of family life? As a college student recently wrote to me from his school in Idaho, "Why would I try to destroy America's family values if those are what I whole-heartedly believe in?"

What most gay and lesbian people *would* like is to be accepted by their families as full and equal members; they would like the definition of family to be broadened to include the realities of American family life—a reality that includes gay and lesbian families of all kinds.

- ## How do parents react to a gay or lesbian child?

How parents react to a lesbian daughter or gay son has a lot to do with who the parents are: their backgrounds, the communities they come from, their ethnic or racial groups, whether or not they're deeply religious, and so forth. But no matter how open-minded parents are—even if half their friends are gay, or they already have one gay child, or are actively involved in working for gay rights—parents are almost universally upset when they find out their son or daughter is gay.

Parents are likely to have a range of reactions, including shock, tears, denial, disappointment, guilt, and quite possibly anger and hostility. They may hope that this is just a phase, or they may wonder what they did wrong, or they may express concern about AIDS, or they may think that this is an attempt to punish them in some way. Their reactions may have nothing to do with reality, but when it comes to facing the fact that a child is gay or lesbian, parents react based on the myths and stereotypes we all grew up with.

Many parents, though upset by the news that a child is gay or lesbian, manage to deal with it in a loving way. Andrea's mother and father reacted to the news that she was a lesbian with tears. "They weren't the only ones crying," said Andrea, who said she is closer to her parents now than before she came out to them. "There was a lot they didn't understand, and I know this isn't what they wanted for me, but as much as they were hurting, they managed to tell me that I was their daughter and they loved me. There are still times when it isn't easy. Like the first time I brought my girlfriend home for dinner, they were really nervous. But, then, Penny and I were really nervous, too."

Not all parents who react with tears go on to state their love for their gay or lesbian child. Karen, a junior high school teacher, also cried when her twenty-seven-year-old son, Alex, told her that he was gay, but she had no reassuring words for her son, because her tears weren't about her concern for her son or even tears of disappointment. Karen was crying because she felt betrayed and was furious. "I wanted him dead, and I told him so. As far as I was concerned he was dead. He was out of my life." To Karen, the son she had known died in that moment of revelation. And she was not at all happy with her "new" son.

As strong as Karen's reaction was, some parents react far more harshly. Kevin was seventeen and still living with his parents when they found out he was gay. "I didn't tell them, because I knew they'd flip out. They're totally into the church, so to them being gay is the most incredibly sinful thing you can do. But I guess they suspected something, because they searched my room and found this note from my boyfriend. You should have seen the look on my father's face when I got home from school. I thought he would kill me." In fact, Kevin's father almost broke Kevin's arm before throwing him out of the house. In the year since then, despite several attempts to contact his parents, Kevin's mother and father have refused to have anything to do with him.

Fortunately, Alex's and Kevin's experiences are not universal. And in Alex's case, after six months, his mother began calling almost every day asking him to forgive her and to come home for Thanksgiving.

What is often hardest for parents with a gay or lesbian child to cope with is a sense of embarrassment and/or fear of what friends, neighbors, relatives, or even strangers will think if they find out. Paradoxically, though a gay son or lesbian daughter who comes out of the closet is now free of the burden of hiding the truth, parents most often find themselves in a closet of their own, hiding the truth about their gay or lesbian child. Every time they're faced with a question like, "Is your son married?" or "Is your daughter dating anyone?" parents have to decide what to say.

In the few years since Karen's son Alex came out to her, she has told several of her friends and a handful of colleagues that her son is gay. All, thus far, have been supportive, but she's still having a hard time. "Hardly a day goes by when one of the other teachers doesn't come bouncing into school talking about a new grandchild. 'Don't worry, this will happen to you soon,' they tell me. I used to run out to the bathroom and cry. Others say, 'The worst thing that could happen would be if my child were a homosexual.' I don't want their pity or rejection. I know I shouldn't feel this way. I should grow up, but that's how I feel. And I'm terrified of having my students find out. Almost every day they call each other *fag*. Of course I feel compelled to scold them. If only they knew."

For my own mother, it was years before she felt comfortable telling the full truth about me. "I know a lot of parents feel they did something wrong," she told me, "and that people will blame them for raising a gay child, so they don't say anything because they fear being judged. But that wasn't the case with me. I was disappointed and confused, but I still didn't want anyone to know. I felt that if anyone knew, then you would be stigmatized, rejected, looked at as defective or inferior. Somehow I couldn't bear the thought of someone judging you. Before I knew you were gay, I always thought of you as someone very special. After I knew, I didn't see how you could have a full life, how you could be anything but an outsider. You were no longer the son I knew. I don't know if I was ashamed, but I was no longer proud of my son."

Years later, after my mother realized I was not defective and was the same son as I was before, she grew more accustomed to answering truthfully, but the reactions people had were nonetheless embarrassing and upsetting. "When your first book was published [*The Male Couple's Guide*], I brought it to a family dinner. I was very proud and wanted to show it to those who were present. I started to speak about the book, but before I said what it was about, some relatives at the table asked to see it, and when it came into their hands, they looked at it, never said a word, and changed the subject. It was as if someone smacked me in the face. I realized that for some people it wasn't even a subject to be spoken about."

My mom sees that family dinner as her turning point. "After that, I refused to hide my son. If I spoke about my children, I had to speak about all my children, their lives, the fact that two were married, and that one was gay and in a relationship, otherwise I would have been ashamed of myself for hiding. Parents who are still ashamed of their gay and lesbian children need to look at why they're not questioning what they've been told by society. Most of our children are healthy, decent, caring, sensitive people, and we fail them when we join the rest of society in denying who they are. We are their parents. If we don't defend their right to live full lives, who will?"

■ Do mothers and fathers react differently from each other to a gay or lesbian child?

Mothers and fathers may react differently to a gay or lesbian child, but not consistently enough to generalize that fathers always have more trouble with their gay sons or mothers always have more trouble with their lesbian daughters. It is safe to say, however, that mothers and fathers often have different expectations for their children depending on whether that child is a boy or a girl, and that their reactions to a child's homosexuality may be tied to these differing expectations. For example, Richard Ashworth, the father of two gay sons and one straight son and a very active long-time member of Parents and Friends of Lesbians and Gays (P-FLAG), said, "Fathers train males to be macho. So being a 'he-man' is a very important thing. Fathers may expect to live their lack of success in that area through their children. I think [with a gay son] you may find more disappointment from the father at first. I don't think you find that as much in a mother."

■ What should you do if you think your child is gay or lesbian?
■ What should you do if you find out that your child is gay?

If you think your child is gay or lesbian, or if you've just found out that your child is gay or lesbian, you need to find the appropriate way to handle your specific circumstances. That means talking to other parents who have gay kids and reading whatever useful material you can get your hands on. The best place to start is with the local chapter of the Federation of Parents and Friends of Lesbians and Gays (P-FLAG), where you can talk with other parents who have gay and lesbian children and can get personal, specific advice on what to do in your situation. To receive printed information, you can call or write P-FLAG's national headquarters:

P-FLAG
P.O. Box 27605
Washington, DC 20038
202-638-4200

■ How do grandparents react to a gay grandchild?

"Whatever you do, don't tell the grandparents!" "They're old. They'll never understand. They don't need to know. Let them die in peace." "You're their favorite. Why destroy their image of you?" These are the kinds of exhortations from well-meaning family members that many gay and lesbian people confront when they bring up the possibility of sharing the truth about their lives with the grandparents. And though the grandparents, like the parents, are likely to greet the news of a gay grandchild with surprise, grandparents often prove to be more resilient and more accepting than parents for all the same reasons grandparents are almost always more accepting of what their grandchildren do than of what their own children do.

Bob and Elaine Benov, who are active members of the Federation of Parents and Friends of Lesbians and Gays, told me my favorite story involving grandparents. Bob waited until a couple of years after his son came out to talk with his own parents—the grandparents—about his son's homosexuality: "I went to visit them at home and told them I had something to talk to them about. My mother asked if there was anything wrong. I told her that nothing was wrong but there was something I wanted to talk to them about. So I said, 'You know all those Sundays when you wanted to come visit or you wanted Elaine and me to come here, and I said I had business appointments? We never had business appointments. Elaine and I are members of an organization, and we go to meetings. The organization is for parents of gays.' I stopped at that point, but they didn't react. So I asked, 'Do you know what *gay* is, Mom?' And my mother looked at me. 'Sure, that's when a guy likes a guy.' And I added, 'Yeah, and when a girl likes a girl.' 'Oh,' she said, 'the girls do it, too?'

"So I proceeded to explain homosexuality. They said, 'That's fine.' And I said, 'The reason we go to the meetings is that one of our sons is gay.' My mother said, 'Oh, we've known that for a long time.' I looked at them, and my mouth fell open in awe. So I asked her which of my sons they thought was gay. And they said Jonathan. I said, 'You're right, but what made you think Jonathan was gay?' 'Well,' my mother said, 'when he talks his voice squeaks, and he uses his hands a lot when he talks.' I said, 'Mom, that has nothing to do with being gay.' I explained a bit more, and at some point they commented, 'They're entitled to everything in life just like everyone else.'"

Not all grandparents are as matter-of-fact as the Benovs, but it's important to remember that grandparents are not nearly as fragile, uninformed, or unwilling to learn about new things as we may think.

■ What should you tell a child who has a gay uncle or aunt?

What you say depends on the age of the child, the circumstances, and the questions a child asks. For example, David has a young niece and nephew. He's been with his lover, Lew, since before the children were born. "From the time they could speak," said David, "they called us Uncle David and Uncle Lew. To them it seemed like the most natural thing in the world. I'm sure that when they get older and notice that most couples are male and female, they'll have some questions about their two uncles. I've already talked with my brother and sister-in-law about this, and they plan to say that sometimes two men love each other just like Mommy and Daddy love each other. I don't think the kids will have any problem with that. The problems may come up later when they start hearing things about *fags* at school. But we'll deal with that when the time comes."

▪ Do gay people want to have children?

Like heterosexual people, many gay and lesbian people want to be parents, and for all the same reasons. For example, David and Lew knew they wanted to be parents even before they met. "I come from a large, happy family," said David. "Early on I saw the importance of being in a family environment. Since my nephew and niece were born and since many of my friends have had children, I've seen how emotionally rewarding it can be. And as I've gotten older, my paternal instincts have gotten very strong." David and Lew are still exploring their options for having children.

Cynthia and Helen, who have two children, both through artificial insemination, knew from the start of their relationship that children were a part of the long-term plan. "When I pictured what my life would be like," Helen explained, "the picture always included kids. That never changed, even after I realized I was a lesbian. I just knew that I had to find a lover who felt the same way. I made very clear to Cynthia when we first started seeing each other that I wanted children, and fortunately she felt the same way I did. Well, maybe not exactly the same, but by the time we actually did it, Cynthia was just as committed and enthusiastic as I was."

- # Do gay and lesbian people have children? How can they?
- # Can gay and lesbian people, or couples, adopt?

Many gay men and lesbians have children, although most gay people who are parents became parents while they were involved in heterosexual marriages. However, a growing number of gay people, particularly lesbian couples, are choosing to have children through a variety of methods, including artificial insemination, adoption, co-parenting, and surrogacy.

For single lesbians and lesbian couples, the most popular way to have a child has been through artificial insemination, using either sperm from an anonymous donor or sperm from a known donor. The Lambda Legal Defense and Education Fund, a legal organization that works to advance the rights of lesbians and gay men through test-case litigation, estimates that there are ten thousand children in the United States being reared by lesbians who conceived through donor insemination. Gay men and male couples most often go the adoption route.

Some gay and lesbian people have also chosen to have children through surrogacy or co-parenting arrangements. In its simplest terms, surrogacy involves a man contracting with a woman to have a baby using his sperm. Following the birth of the child, the birth mother gives up the child, and the man becomes the child's parent. Co-parenting can involve two to four parents. For example, a lesbian couple and a male couple may arrange for one of the men to donate his sperm to impregnate one of the two women. The four parents then share custody of the child according to whatever agreement they've worked out. Both of these methods for having children require, among other things, very sound legal advice and detailed contracts.

For gay and lesbian couples, the most significant legal problem with most of these methods is the issue of custody. For example, if a male couple chooses to adopt a child, only one of the two men can legally adopt the child, because most states forbid adoption by unmarried couples. The second father has no legal rights to that child should the adoptive father die or the couple separate. Or if a lesbian couple chooses to have a child using anonymous donor sperm, only the woman who bears the child is the legal parent; the second mother, who cannot legally marry the child's biological mother, is not permitted to adopt the child.

Fortunately, a handful of recent precedent-setting cases have allowed "second parent" adoptions. One of these cases involved two women in New York, Valerie C., the biological mother of Evan, a six-year-old boy, and her life partner, Diane F. Together, who've raised Evan since his birth. The court granted the second parent adoption to Diane on January 30, 1992, and stated in its ruling, "Today a child who receives proper nutrition, adequate schooling, and supportive, sustaining shelter is among the fortunate, whatever the source. A child who also receives the love and nurture of even a single parent can be counted among the blessed. Here this court finds a child who has all of the above benefits and *two* adults dedicated to his welfare, secure in their loving partnership, and determined to raise him to the very best of their considerable abilities. There is no reason in law, logic, or social philosophy to obstruct such a favorable situation."

- **Why do some people object to gay people having children?**
- **Do gay parents raise gay children?**

The common myths about gay and lesbian parents—and I emphasize the word *myths*—that are often expressed by those who oppose gay and lesbian people having, adopting, and raising children, are that they are more likely to molest their children, that they will raise gay and lesbian children, that children raised by two parents of the same sex will be poorly adjusted, and that the children of gay parents will be discriminated against.

First, gay and lesbian people are no more likely to sexually abuse their children than heterosexual people (and as the study I cite in chapter 1 from the Children's Hospital in Denver suggests, gay and lesbian parents are far less likely to do so). Second, you cannot intentionally raise a gay child any more than you can intentionally raise a heterosexual child. From everything that is known, a parent cannot affect a child's sexual orientation. Third, whether or not a child is well adjusted has more to do with whether or not a child is loved than whether there are two mothers, two fathers, a mother and a father, or a single parent.

The one argument against gay and lesbian people raising children that is based in fact is that the children of gay and lesbian people are likely to face special challenges because of society's prejudice against gay men and lesbians. It is true that the children of gay and lesbian people may feel they have to hide the fact that their parents are gay or may have to contend with prejudiced remarks or negative reactions from their friends or the parents of their friends who don't approve of gay and lesbian people. But this is no more a rational argument against gay and lesbian people having children than it would be for any other group that faces discrimination in our society. This is, however, a good argument for working to change people's negative attitudes.

- **What happens when gay or lesbian couples who have kids split up?**
- **Who gets the child(ren)?**
- **Are there visitation rights?**
- **What happens when one parent dies?**

Many gay and lesbian couples, like heterosexual couples, split up. And when kids are involved it can be especially complicated, because for most gay and lesbian couples who have children, only one parent is the legal parent (adoptive or biological).

When gay and lesbian couples in this situation can agree on custody arrangements—which, ideally, they have put in writing prior to having the child—then there are no problems beyond the usual challenges divorced couples with children face. But when a gay or lesbian couple who have a child can't agree on custody arrangements, and only one parent is the legal parent, then the other parent will find he or she has no legal rights. This was the case with Nancy S. and Michele G., who lived together from 1969 to 1985. As it was reported in 1991 by the Associated Press, in 1980 Nancy gave birth to a daughter and in 1984 a son, both through artificial insemination. Michele was listed on the birth certificates as the father and gave the children her last name. When the couple separated, they agreed that each child would live with one woman five days a week.

For the next three years, the daughter spent five days a week with Michele, and the son spent five days a week with Nancy. For the remaining two days, the women exchanged children. At the end of the third year, Nancy sought half the time with each child. When Michele refused, Nancy sued and won a ruling from the Alameda County Superior Court in California granting her sole custody of both children, with no visitation rights for Michele.

The same year as the California decision, New York's Court of Appeals decided that a lesbian could not seek visiting rights to the child of her former partner, a child the two women raised from birth until the child was three years old. The court wrote that state law restricts visiting rights to parents and other blood relatives of children, like siblings and grandparents. The ruling went on to state, "We decline to read the term *parent* to include categories of non-parents who have devel-

oped a relationship with a child or who have had prior relationships with a child's parents and who wish to continue visitation with the child."

For couples in which both parents are legal parents—that is,
both have legally adopted the child, or one is the biological parent and the other is a legal adoptive parent—there is plenty of
legal precedent to be followed should the parents be unable to
agree on custody arrangements.

In the event a parent dies, the surviving parent will retain
custody of the child or children as long as that parent is the biological or legal adoptive parent. If the surviving partner is not
the biological or legal adoptive parent, the outcome can be di-
sastrous, because in the eyes of the law that parent has no legal
relationship with the child. If the second parent wishes to gain
custody of the child or children, he or she will face a difficult
legal battle to gain custody, particularly if the child or children's legal next of kin wish to assume custody.

- ## Is it better to tell children about a homosexual parent or hide the truth?
- ## What's the best time to tell children?

I believe that if it's at all possible it's best to be honest
about your homosexuality with your children. I think that
family secrets are poison, whatever their nature. But that's my
opinion. I've talked to parents who insist that I'm right, and
I've talked to parents who insist that I'm wrong and that it's
none of my business.

Sometimes parents must keep their homosexuality a secret
from their children because of necessity. If a parent is em-
broiled in a custody battle in which the sexual orientation of
the parent could affect the outcome, then hiding the truth is
essential. For parents who are not faced with this kind of

dilemma, whether or not they share this information with their children is a matter of personal choice.

What parents choose to do depends on many different things, including their specific circumstances. For example, if an openly gay male or lesbian couple is raising a child together from infancy, they are not likely to hide the nature of their relationship from their child and will therefore have nothing to disclose. The child will have observed her parents as a couple—being affectionate, sharing a bed—and will over time become aware that they are gay or lesbian.

For a parent who has left a heterosexual marriage, it's a matter of deciding whether or not to tell a child that his parent is something different from what he thought he was. If the gay or lesbian parent has custody of that child, it could be very difficult to hide the truth, especially if the parent is actively dating or has a lover. Kids aren't stupid, and if there's a secret to be found out, they'll make every effort to uncover the truth. If, on the other hand, the parent does not have custody and the child visits only during designated times, it is easier to hide the truth.

For those parents who choose to come out to their children, the rule of thumb is, the sooner the better. That was what Lloyd, a father of a teenaged son and daughter, learned from other gay fathers he met through a local support group. "I found out that the younger the children, the easier it was. Especially before they were teens and dealing with their own sexuality and were more aware about sexual things and had peer pressure. When they're younger, they're more accepting of things. They're not even so sure what gay is. They just want to know that their father is still their father."

Joy Schulenburg, a lesbian mom and the author of *Gay Parenting*, concurs that children deal better with the news that a parent is gay when they're still young: "Among the children I talked to and corresponded with, there were distinct differences in attitudes between those who had been under twelve when they learned their parent was gay and those who had been twelve and over. The under-twelve age group seemed largely indifferent to their parent's sexual orientation (which is true also of children of heterosexuals). Most of them simply didn't understand what all the fuss was about. Parents were loved because they were parents, despite any personal quirks and without reservations. Once puberty set in, with its sexual awakening and attending social pressures, reactions varied and the incidence of concern and initial rejection increased."

■ How do children react to homosexual parents?

How children react to a parent's homosexuality depends to a large degree on when they find out a parent is gay. For a child who has been raised since birth or early childhood by two parents of the same sex, the awareness is evolutionary. At first the child may only be aware that she has two parents of the same sex who sleep in the same bed. Eventually she will realize that her other friends have parents of the opposite sex and will likely ask her parents why she has two daddies or two mommies instead of a mommy and a daddy. Then she'll learn the words for what her parents are and gain a fuller understanding of what this means. For a child like this, there is no one moment of revelation when a child discovers that her supposedly heterosexual parent is gay. So for this child there is no real news to react to.

When children are raised by a mother and father, and later one of the parents comes out of the closet, children react in a variety of ways, from shock and rejection to relief that their parent has finally confirmed what they already knew. Children may also be concerned about the possibility of a gay father contracting AIDS.

Some parents have had terrible experiences, like one woman I know whose devoutly religious teenage daughter refused to ever see her again. Other parents have had very positive experiences, like a man I know whose two sons just wanted to be certain that their father still loved them. Lloyd, the father of two children, said that what he learned from his own experience and the experiences of other gay fathers he knows was that "in almost all cases when the kids found out, it was okay. This was their father; he was gay. They would have some problems but would eventually come around."

Ann Northrop, who has been a stepmother to her lover's two sons, concluded from her experience that the way children ultimately respond to their parents' homosexuality has a great deal to do with the kind of relationship the parents have with their children. "The secret really turns out to be, do you have a loving relationship with your kids? And if you love and respect them, they tend to love and respect you. It's something that needs a lot of attention and work and commitment, like any relationship."

■ What kinds of special problems do children of gay parents have?

The world is not a very friendly place for gay and lesbian people, and that makes it a challenging place for their children as well. Nonetheless, as reported by Daniel Goleman in the *New York Times* in December 1992, "According to a review of new studies in the current issue of the journal *Child Development*, children raised by gay parents are no more likely to have psychological problems than those raised in more conventional circumstances. While they may face teasing or even ridicule, especially in adolescence, the studies show that, over all, there are no psychological disadvantages for children . . . being raised by homosexuals."

As reported in the article, one of the studies, which was conducted by Dr. Julie Gottman, a clinical psychologist in Seattle, found that as a group, the children of lesbians did not differ from children of heterosexual mothers in their social adjustment or their identity as a boy or a girl. And the children of lesbians were no more likely to be homosexual than those of heterosexual mothers. Dr. Gottman said, "What mattered most for their adjustment was whether the mother had a partner in the home, whether male or female. If so, those children tended to do somewhat better than the others in self-confidence, self-acceptance, and independence. But the sexual orientation of the lesbian mothers had no adverse affects." According to the article, that conclusion "was confirmed by about three dozen studies reviewed in *Child Development* by Charlotte Patterson, a psychologist at the University of Virginia."

■ What do kids call their two same-sex parents?

What may be a perplexing dilemma for an adult who is trying to imagine how a child figures out what to call two mommies or two daddies has been no problem for the kids I've talked to. Susan, who is ten, calls her fathers, who have raised her since birth, Papa Don and Daddy David. Michael, who is twenty-four, calls his natural father Dad and his father's lover who raised Michael, Mama Chuck. (Mind you, Mama Chuck is over six feet four inches tall and weighs 250 pounds.) Ellen and Doug, who are in their twenties, call their mother Mom and their mother's lover, whom she's been with for the last ten years, by her first name.

5

DATING

- **How do gay people meet?**

    When Barbara, a clerk-typist from Philadelphia, was a young woman back in the early 1950s, she desperately wanted to meet other women who were gay. Until then, she had only read about lesbians in novels. "I don't remember exactly how I knew about gay bars, probably from all the reading I'd done, but somehow I heard about a bar in New York City. To save money on bus fare, I hitchhiked to New York from where I lived in Philadelphia—this was obviously a long time ago. When I finally found the place and found my people, it was marvelous. I don't like bars, but I was thrilled to meet people who were like me."

Though these bars were just about the only place gay men and lesbians could go in the 1950s to meet other people they knew were gay, today in every major and midsize city, gay and lesbian people meet in a variety of settings, from gay and lesbian running clubs and softball teams to religious organizations and volunteer groups—in addition to bars, restaurants, and clubs that cater specifically to a gay and lesbian clientele. But these aren't the only places and the only ways gay and lesbian people meet each other. Just like everyone else, gay and lesbian people meet at work, at social events, and at the grocery store and are introduced through friends and even family. When I was in my early twenties and single, my mother and her friend Fran decided their gay sons should meet. They figured if they weren't going to have daughters-in-law of any kind, they might as well try for Jewish sons-in-law. (It was a nice try, but we didn't make it past the second date.)

■ How do gay people spot each other?

Figuring out if the man or woman you're interested in dating is in fact gay or lesbian is often no small challenge. Unless you meet in a setting where you know for sure that everyone is gay, you're left in the difficult position of trying to figure it out. I remember once in college telling my friend Mary Ann about an upperclassman I had a crush on. Every time I mentioned his name over a period of several days, Mary Ann said, "I don't think he's interested in men." The more Mary Ann tried to dissuade me, the more I insisted that he was gay. Finally, I listed all my reasons for believing that John was gay. I told Mary Ann, "He's sensitive; he seems to enjoy my company; he takes good care of himself. There's just something about him. I know he's gay." Mary Ann rolled her eyes and said, "I'm *sure* he's not." I asked her how she could be so certain, and she looked at me as if she couldn't believe how dense

I was and said, "Because I've been sleeping with him for the past month!" I was so grateful that I hadn't asked him out on a date! The last thing I wanted to do was make a pass at a straight guy.

Sometimes it's relatively easy to figure out if the man or woman you've taken a liking to is gay. For example, if he or she is wearing a button or jewelry that indicates support for gay causes. Another clue might be if his or her style of clothing or haircut conforms to what's popular among gay and lesbian people. But if there are no outward signs, then it can be a major challenge. If you're in a business situation, for example, you may have to be very careful, beyond all the usual reasons you have to be careful about pursuing romantic interests at the office. If you've kept your sexual orientation a secret from your colleagues, you have to feel confident that the person you're interested in is also gay or lesbian—and in addition will protect your secret. The last thing you want to do in a case like this is reveal the fact you're gay to someone who will blow your cover. So you have to proceed very carefully.

When Jane met Justine in the company cafeteria, it was love at first sight, but Jane had no idea whether or not Justine was gay. She had her hopes, especially when Justine gave her a broad smile when they met, but she couldn't be sure. Over the next couple of weeks Jane gathered evidence from their conversations. "I found out that Justine lived alone. She never talked about boyfriends. Her politics seemed on target. But it wasn't until I met her at her apartment one evening to go to the movies that I was absolutely sure. Her books were a dead giveaway." Of course, Justine was also gathering evidence, so by the time she invited Jane to meet her at her apartment before the movie, she was confident that Jane was also gay. "I could tell from the way she looked at me. Jane may have thought she was being subtle, but if there's one thing Jane isn't, it's subtle!"

▪ What do gay people do on a date?

Whether it's the first date or the tenth, what gay people do on dates varies as much as what heterosexual people do on dates. On my first date with a man, when I was seventeen, Bob and I went to see a movie about two young men who had fallen in love. During the movie Bob and I held hands, but I waited for the lights to go down before I searched for Bob's hand because I was afraid of what people might say if they saw what we were doing. Scott and Mark had planned to drive to the beach for their fifth date, but they never got out of the house. For Cynthia and Debbie, their first date started with dinner on Debbie's terrace overlooking the Pacific Ocean in Santa Monica.

▪ Who makes the first move? Who drives? Who pays?

Debbie's first date with Cynthia went really well. Dinner was wonderful. There was plenty to talk about. Both were feeling very romantic by the time they had finished dessert and coffee and were standing at the railing of Debbie's terrace watching the sun set over the Pacific. Debbie wanted to kiss Cynthia. And Cynthia wanted to kiss Debbie. "But we were both waiting for the other to make the first move!" explained Debbie. "Both of us were pretty new to dating women, and growing up you learn that the boy is supposed to make the first move. But finally after standing there looking at each other for a while, not knowing what to do, we just started laughing because we realized why we were just standing there and not doing what we both wanted to do. So we just went for it. After the first kiss, whoever felt like making the first move did. Well, it wasn't always that simple, but we tried to do what we felt like doing and not what we thought we should do based on the fact we're women and the roles we're taught to play."

When you're two women or two men in a dating situation, you don't just fall into the standard boy-girl roles, unless you're both comfortable choosing compatible roles. For most gay and lesbian people, who makes the first move, who drives, who pays for the date, who makes the first call, and so forth are dictated by many different factors that are often not nearly as simple and clear-cut as the standard boy-girl routine that heterosexual people can choose to follow. So who pays for dinner may depend on who asked whom out for the date or who makes more money. Or you may agree that you always go dutch. The one who reaches across the table to make the first kiss may simply be the one who is feeling more confident at a given moment. And the one who drives may be the one who prefers to drive. But, of course, gay people aren't the only ones who face the challenge—and opportunity—of undefined roles. Roles for heterosexuals are not nearly as well defined as they once were.

■ What do you do if you are heterosexual and you think the man or woman you are dating is gay?

First you have to think about what it is that makes you think the person you're dating is gay or lesbian. My friend Tina said that some of her friends think that a man is gay if he won't have sex on the first date. "Plenty of straight men don't want to go to bed on the first date. Most often it has nothing to do with whether or not a guy likes women. I don't understand what the rush is. Once you've crossed that line, there's no going back. And it's also possible that the guy you're dating just doesn't find you all that physically interesting. That's a hard one to accept."

But sometimes a lack of interest in sex may indeed be an indicator that your boyfriend or girlfriend is gay or lesbian. If you feel that the man or woman you're dating doesn't have a lot of interest in the opposite sex, you can try asking him or her, "What is the problem?" If you're comfortable, you can ask bluntly, "Are you gay?" but that won't necessarily elicit an honest response. If my first girlfriend in college had asked me if I was gay, I would have said no—not because I was trying to hide anything, but because I hadn't even admitted it to myself. Although Anna never asked me, I learned from her years later that she was pretty sure I was gay because of my lack of interest in doing anything physical other than kissing, and I don't remember being very enthusiastic about that either.

If you can't get what you feel is an honest response from the man or woman you're dating, you may find that your only alternative is to end the dating relationship. That doesn't mean you can't be friends, but there is no reason to subject yourself to a relationship with someone who would really rather be with a person of the same sex.

6

RELATIONSHIPS AND MARRIAGE

- ## Do gay people have couple relationships?

Not long ago, I had a talk about relationships with my best friend's dad. We had just come from dinner with my best friend and his (male) spouse of seven years. We got into a conversation about the ups and downs of long-term relationships, and my friend's dad said, "One of the things I've learned as I've gotten to know gay people is that people are people, love is love, and relationships are relationships, whether it's two men, two women, or a man and a woman."

Because he now knows several gay and lesbian people, including a number of couples, my friend's father has had the opportunity to see that gay and lesbian people have relationships that are full of all the joy, excitement, challenge, and satisfaction, as well as hurt, disappointment, and tragedy, that heterosexuals experience.

■ How long do gay and lesbian couple relationships last?

Gay and lesbian couple relationships, like heterosexual couple relationships, can last anywhere from a matter of days to a half-century or more. But because gay and lesbian people remain largely hidden, there are no accurate statistics on the number of gay and lesbian couples or the average length of these relationships.

■ Are there more gay and lesbian couples now than in years past? Why?

In all likelihood, there are more gay and lesbian couples now than in the past, probably many more, and there are several reasons why, from changing expectations to more varied opportunities to meet potential partners.

Until very recently, the prevailing myth about gay and lesbian relationships was that they couldn't possibly last. Even though old myths die hard, most gay and lesbian people now know that it's possible to have a relationship, and many actively pursue that possibility.

Finding a potential partner is now easier than it was in the past. First, there are more and more openly gay and lesbian people out there to choose from. Second, there are many more places to meet, from religious groups to professional organizations.

Many gay and lesbian couples can now also count on the kind of familial, religious, social, and even legal support that heterosexual couples take for granted. For example, when

Brent and Tom gave a party for their tenth anniversary, Brent's parents and sister were an important part of the celebration. "Both sets of parents are very supportive of our relationship," said Brent. "Tom's parents would have been there, but they're quite a bit older than my parents, and the trip was just too much for them. But they called and sent a gift." Tom and Brent have also formalized their relationship with a religious "union" ceremony at their local church and with a Domestic Partnership certificate offered by the City of San Francisco to unmarried couples. (For more on domestic partnerships, see "What can gay couples do to approximate marriage laws?" later in this chapter.)

■ Are there more gay male couples because of AIDS?

There are writers, journalists, and trend watchers who have suggested that AIDS forced the generation of gay men who grew up in the relatively wild 1970s to "mature and settle down."

Though the impact of AIDS on gay men has been severe, I don't think AIDS is a significant factor in the growing numbers of gay male couples. I do think that AIDS has revealed how common couple relationships are among gay men, however. Through television and magazine stories, as well as newspaper articles and obituaries, we have all learned that many gay men have longtime companions, not to mention loving friends and even loving and supportive families.

■ What do gay and lesbian people call their companions?

In one of her first nationally syndicated columns for the *Detroit News*, Deb Price wrote about the problem lesbian and gay people face when introducing a partner, spouse, lover, significant other, special friend, longtime companion, wife, husband, boyfriend, girlfriend, life partner, or whatever. As Deb wrote, "Who says the gay rights movement hasn't made a lot of progress? In just 100 years, we've gone from the love that dare not speak its name to the love that doesn't know its name." She asked readers to help her come up with a term that she could use to introduce her partner, Joyce.

The answers Deb got weren't all positive, she wrote in her column a month later. "People who read 'G-A-Y' as 'S-E-X' apparently also misread my question: I didn't ask people to call Joyce names." Deb then listed some of the names writers volunteered: sodomite, partner in sin, and sick. Despite the name-calling, most of those who wrote to Deb had serious suggestions, the best of which Deb decided was "love-mate."

Whatever words gay and lesbian people use for their "love-mates," they often use different words depending on who they're talking to. For example, when Donna talks about Joanna with her colleagues or family, she refers to Joanna as her *spouse* or *partner*. "These are words straight people can easily relate to, and they know what I mean," said Donna. When she talks about Joanna with her lesbian and gay friends, Donna uses either *lover, wife,* or for fun, *the little woman.* She knows that her gay and lesbian friends know *lover* means the same thing as spouse, and that calling Joanna her *wife* doesn't imply that Donna is the husband. "We're two wives," said Donna. "Gay people know what these words mean because we're used to them, but if I talked to my mother about Joanna being my wife, she would look at me like I was crazy."

Daryl and Carlton, who have been a couple for nearly fifteen years, told me my favorite story on this subject. "When Daryl took me to his architecture school graduation dinner party, he introduced me as his 'comrade' to all his professors. Everyone thought we were communists or something. It was embarrassing. By the end of the night I convinced him to use 'spouse.'"

- ## Do gay and lesbian couples have pet names or nicknames for each other?

Like heterosexual couples, gay and lesbian couples over time often develop their own "language." This language—words and phrases that have special meaning only to the individual couple—may include pet names. Over the years I've talked to lesbian and gay people in couple relationships who have affectionately called each other everything from "Bunny" to "Wonkie."

- ## Who plays the husband, and who plays the wife?

When I worked at "CBS This Morning" several years ago, one of my colleagues asked me this question. She was well educated. She knew gay and lesbian people, and she didn't have a prejudiced bone in her body. She was just curious and thought I could answer the question. I answered her question with a question. I asked her who in her relationship—she had been married to a man for several years—played the husband, and who played the wife? I wasn't trying to be glib or sarcastic. I just wanted her to think about the question and how it related to her own life. She smiled, because she knew what I was getting at, and said, "We don't really have traditional husband-wife roles. We both work. We both cook, although my husband is a better cook. We send out the laundry. And we both hate to clean." I then explained that for the gay and lesbian couples I knew it was pretty much the same. Chores didn't fall along traditional husband-wife lines. For example, who made dinner was far more dependent on who got home from work first than on who was more feminine. As for who, if anyone, took the lead in decision making, that just depended on the personalities of the people in the individual relationships, not their gender.

In one of the many classes Ann Northrop has taught to high school students in New York City on the subject of homosexuality, the issue of how lesbian couples made decisions prompted one young man to ask, "Well, if you don't have a guy in the relationship, how do you know who's in charge?" Ann's reply: "Linda and I like to think we have a complementary, but equal relationship, that we do not play roles, but instead, make decisions together. When it comes to chores, we do whatever we're willing to do or able to do. We don't think it takes a penis to carry out the garbage. Linda's mad at me at the moment because she doesn't think I cook enough, and she's probably right. But look at heterosexual relationships. Some have role divisions, some don't."

After relating this story to me, Ann added, "I thought we tried to get rid of this role-playing business twenty years ago."

Like many heterosexual couples, some gay and lesbian couples follow a more traditional husband-wife model. This shouldn't surprise anyone, given that we all grew up with this model for couple relationships. For example, during the first year after a male couple I know adopted an infant boy, one stayed home and took care of the baby and did the shopping, cleaning, and all the cooking. The other partner went to the office and provided the financial support for the whole family. The next year, they switched roles; the one who had worked at an office came home to take care of the baby, and the one who had been taking care of the baby went back to working in an office. This isn't the only possible arrangement. In another couple I met, both women had full-time jobs, but one partner performed the traditional "female" chores, like cleaning the house and cooking, while the other partner took care of the traditional "male" chores, such as mowing the lawn and maintaining the car.

- ### Who brings home flowers?
- ### Who initiates on Valentine's Day?
- ### Who drives?

Even among my most liberated heterosexual couple friends, including couples in which the wives have profoundly successful careers, it's the husbands who bring their wives flowers, the husbands who plan something special for Valentine's Day (or risk being flogged), and the husbands who almost always drive the car.

For gay men and lesbians who are in couple relationships, unless they assume well-defined husband-wife roles, there is no falling back on traditional gender roles to figure out who should be giving whom the flowers and who should be seated behind the wheel. It just depends on individual expectations and preferences.

For example, Joel thinks it's important to celebrate Valentine's Day. And so does Tony, his lover of three years. So every year for the past three years they've thought up surprises for each other. "The first year," explained Tony, "I got home from work early and made a trail of cut out hearts from the front door to the bedroom. So when Joel got home, he followed the trail into the bedroom, where I was waiting. The candles were set out, I had our favorite CD playing—you know, the whole business." Tony, of course, hadn't forgotten about the holiday and surprised Joel with two dozen red roses and a bottle of champagne. "I also had reservations at our favorite restaurant." And what about driving? "I hate to drive, but I'm great at reading maps," said Tony, "and Joel loves to drive, but he never knows where he's going, so it works out well for us."

▪ Who plays the husband and who plays the wife in bed?

For some gay and lesbian couples, one partner routinely takes the passive (or what was traditionally considered the wife's) role and one partner takes the aggressive (or what was traditionally considered the husband's) role. For most gay and lesbian couples, however—and I suspect for many heterosexual couples as well—roles aren't so regimented and may shift back and forth between the partners from minute to minute, hour to hour, day to day. (For more on this subject, see chapter 13, "Sex.")

▪ What are "butch-femme" relationships?

According to Lillian Faderman, as she writes about the butch-femme lesbian subculture in her book *Odd Girls and Twilight Lovers*, some lesbians, primarily young and working class lesbians during the 1950s and 1960s, assumed either masculine ("butch") or feminine ("femme") roles. They expressed these roles in their manner of dress, their demeanor, their sexual behavior, and their choice of partner: butches sought femmes, and femmes hoped to attract butches.

Today, while some lesbian couples and some gay male couples may play traditionally masculine and feminine roles, the strict butch-femme role playing of earlier decades is no longer common.

▪ What kinds of relationship problems do gay and lesbian people have that result from being gay?

All couples, heterosexual and homosexual, face challenges. Gay and lesbian people face some extra challenges, not the least of which is a world that is still fundamentally hostile to same-sex couples. For example, gay and lesbian couples cannot count on the support of family or religious institutions, and gay people are not allowed to legally marry. Besides the legal and financial benefits of marriage, gay and lesbian couples are denied the psychological benefit derived from having their commitment to each other sanctioned and affirmed by the state.

Before gay men and women even get to an age when couple relationships are possible, they have to overcome their own negative feelings about what they are, the result of society's general condemnation of homosexuality. Add to that society's expectation that gay and lesbian relationships can't possibly last, and that gay and lesbian couples have few role models, and it begins to seem miraculous that there are *any* gay and lesbian couples at all.

■ Are male couples monogamous?
■ Are female couples monogamous?

I've met plenty of male couples who are monogamous, and many who are not. Anecdotal evidence and a number of studies (including *American Couples* by Philip Blumstein, Ph.D., and Pepper Schwartz, Ph.D., 1983) suggest that male couples are less frequently monogamous than heterosexual couples. On the other hand, I've met plenty of lesbian couples who are monogamous, and not as many who aren't. Anecdotal evidence and a number of studies (including *The Mendola Report* by Mary Mendola, 1980) suggest that lesbian couples are more frequently monogamous than heterosexual couples.

Some gay and lesbian couples that are not monogamous have formally agreed not to be monogamous and have set rules regarding sexual involvements outside the relationship (e.g., sex outside the relationship only when on business trips). But in other gay and lesbian couples, as in plenty of heterosexual couples, one partner secretly engages in sexual liaisons that his or her partner would not approve of if they were revealed.

▪ Can gay people legally marry?

No state currently permits two people of the same sex to legally marry.

▪ Why are gay people fighting for the legal right to get married?

▪ What advantages are there to a legal marriage?

Gay and lesbian people are fighting for the legal right to marry because they want the same legal protections and financial benefits granted to heterosexual married couples.

The legal protections and benefits of marriage are considerable. In most states, married couples have the legal right to be on each other's insurance and pension plans. Married couples also get special tax exemptions and deductions and are eligible for Social Security survivor's benefits. A married person may inherit property and may have automatic rights of survivorship that avoid inheritance tax. Marriage laws also offer legal protection in the event a relationship comes to an end, providing for an orderly distribution of property.

In the case of death or medical emergency, a spouse is the legal "next of kin," which means that he or she can make all decisions regarding medical care and funeral arrangements. And the next of kin is granted automatic visitation rights. The story of Sharon Kowalski and Karen Thompson tragically demonstrated what lack of these automatic rights means when something goes wrong. After a 1983 car accident, Sharon Kowalski was brain-damaged and quadriplegic. It took her spouse, Karen Thompson, seven years to be named guardian over the objections of Sharon's parents, who said their daughter had never told them she was a lesbian. They also barred Karen from visiting their daughter's nursing home for several years after the accident. What took Karen Thompson seven years would have been granted automatically to a legal husband or wife.

For gay and lesbian couples who are raising children, the fact they can't marry means that only one of the two parents can have legal custody of the child. (Only very rarely are two unmarried people allowed to adopt the same child. For more information on second parent adoptions, see chapter 4, "Family and Children.") In the event a couple separates or the legal parent dies, the nonadoptive parent faces a legal nightmare if he or she wishes to retain custody of the child or even secure visitation rights.

And finally, there is the kind of dilemma faced by a couple like Charlene, who is a United States citizen, and Sandrina, who is French. Shortly after Sandrina arrived in the United States to get her master's degree in English literature, she met Charlene. After six months, they moved in together, hoping they could figure out a way for Sandrina to stay in the United States after she graduated. For a heterosexual couple, marriage would have been a natural solution. If Charlene and Sandrina could marry, then Sandrina would be allowed to live and work in the United States. Sandrina will graduate in a few months and still has no idea what she will do once her student visa expires.

■ Why do people oppose gay marriage, and what are their arguments against it?

I've heard all kinds of arguments against letting gay people marry, from "God created Adam and Eve, not Adam and Steve," to "It will devalue heterosexual marriage and destroy the American family."

First, we live in a constitutional democracy with a strict separation of church and state, not a Christian state governed by the Bible. So whether God created Adam and Eve, Adam and Steve, or any other combination, it should have no bearing on state marriage laws. Second, encouraging stable couple relationships among gay and lesbian people can't help but strengthen American family life. Third, I've never heard a convincing argument that allowing gay and lesbian people to legally marry devalues heterosexual marriage.

What I find interesting is that some of the very same men and women who once condemned gay and lesbian people for having failed relationships and for leading lives of promiscuity are now some of the most outspoken opponents of gay marriage. I imagine they would have opposed gay marriage long ago, but who would have guessed that the rights of gay and lesbian couples would ever become a burning issue?

For those people who believe that gay men and lesbians will never be granted the right to legally marry, it helps to remember that until a 1967 Supreme Court ruling, some states prohibited marriage, sex, or procreation between black people and white people.

- ### What can gay couples do to approximate marriage laws?

- ### What about these new domestic partnership laws?

There are several legal documents that gay and lesbian couples can complete that give them some of the legal rights granted to heterosexual married couples. These include a will; a durable power of attorney, which allows you to designate an individual as the person you want to make medical and financial decisions for you should you become incapacitated; and joint ownership agreements. You can also draw up a legal letter, which my attorney calls a "Designation of Preference," in which you state, for example, that you want your partner to be the first person to visit you should you be confined to an intensive care unit. A hospital does not have to honor a "Designation of Preference" letter, but the letter, along with the support of your doctor, may just do the trick.

There is another legal document that is being offered by several cities across the country to nonmarried couples, both heterosexual and homosexual. It's called a Domestic Partnership agreement. In San Francisco, for example, couples who choose to register their relationships with the city through a Domestic Partnership certificate declare that they have "an intimate, committed relationship of mutual caring," that they live together and that they agree to be responsible for each other's basic living expenses. Though the Domestic Partnership certificate is largely symbolic—only states have the right to issue marriage licenses—some couples have attempted to use it to gain family benefits for gay and lesbian spouses from employers, insurance companies, and even health clubs.

■ What kinds of ceremonies do gay and lesbian couples have to celebrate their commitment to each other? Why do they do it?

Because there is no wedding tradition for gay and lesbian couples, there is no one way that they celebrate their commitment to each other. That doesn't mean gay and lesbian couples don't celebrate their commitment; it just means the range of celebrations is very broad, from couples who exchange rings in private to couples who pull out all the stops, including the church ceremony, matching tuxedos or dresses, traditional vows, formal reception for two hundred, and a four-tiered wedding cake topped with two grooms or two brides.

Gay and lesbian couples who choose religious union ceremonies are having less and less difficulty finding ministers or
other mainstream religious leaders to officiate, but that doesn't
mean congregations always welcome gay and lesbian union
ceremonies in their houses of worship. Leslie and Karen had
hoped to hold their union ceremony in the church they attended together for five years in San Diego. "But when push
came to shove," said Leslie, "the majority of the congregation
really didn't want us to do it. Before they made a formal decision, we decided to have the ceremony in our own home. We
didn't want anything to spoil what for us was a very, very important and happy occasion."

The decision of various ministers and rabbis to conduct religious union ceremonies for gay and lesbian couples has led to
widespread debate as well as well-publicized confrontations
across religious denominations.

Until recently, I had never attended a gay wedding or union
ceremony. But last spring I received an invitation to a union ceremony for two of my closest friends. The two men, both in their
late twenties, had been together for nearly three years and formally engaged for a year (they bought each other identical
watches for their engagement). The invitation stated that Bill
and Henry wanted me to join them for a ceremony celebrating
their commitment to each other. The invitation went beyond
the usual date, place, and time to explain what would happen at
the ceremony. "We knew that most of the people we invited had
never been to a gay union ceremony before," explained Henry.
"We thought that the best way to make them comfortable was
to spell out in the invitation what to expect. So in the invitation
we said there would be an exchange of vows and rings, readings
by several different people, and then a reception."

I don't know quite what I expected, but Bill and Henry's ceremony, which they held in their new apartment, was the most
moving "wedding" I've ever been to. (I've put *wedding* in

quotes because Bill and Henry didn't call it a wedding, but in almost all ways, except for the fact the two men couldn't get a marriage license, that's what it was.) Bill and Henry conducted the ceremony themselves. They were flanked on either side by their parents. Both stated their love for each other and their mutual commitment before exchanging traditional gold wedding bands. Then Henry's mother and father spoke, as did Bill's father. By this time I was crying, as were most of the fifty people—friends, family, neighbors, both straight and gay—packed into Bill and Henry's living room. It was an incredibly emotional and loving ceremony, especially as various friends and family came up to speak. Then we all congratulated the dazed couple and feasted on Chinese food. The next day they left for their honeymoon.

I wasn't quite sold on the importance of a union ceremony before I attended Bill and Henry's ceremony. But it was clear to me from that event that the two men had entered a new stage of life—as do all married couples—by stating their vows and love for each other in the company of those people most important to them. And it wasn't just my imagination that things were different for Bill and Henry after their union ceremony. "Our parents treat us differently," said Bill. "There's no question now in their minds that we're a couple, and they don't hesitate to offer their advice, as they would to any married child and his spouse. Sometimes that's good, and sometimes that's not so good." Henry added, "The two of us also take the relationship even more seriously than we did before. It gives us a new sense of commitment and security. It was physically and emotionally exhausting, but I'm glad we did it."

Gay and lesbian couples have many different reasons for having union ceremonies, but most mirror those of heterosexual couples, whether the ceremony is an opportunity to formalize a commitment to each other or a plain and simple celebration of mutual love.

- ## Can gay and lesbian people place wedding announcements in the newspaper?

I wouldn't put money on when the *New York Times* will first publish gay and lesbian wedding announcements, but on March 23, 1991, the *Times* reported that the *Star Tribune* of Minneapolis "broke ground for metropolitan newspapers... when it published two announcements of lesbian 'domestic partnerships' on what had traditionally been its wedding and engagement page." The *Times* also reported that several smaller newspapers on the West Coast had recently adopted similar policies.

- ## For gay and lesbian people in couple relationships, when you fill out a registration form at a doctor's office, for example, do you check the box for "married" or "single"?

Some gay and lesbian people in couple relationships check "married," and some check "single." When faced with a form that doesn't offer any other options, one lesbian friend of mine writes in "lesbian couple," draws a box next to it, and checks it off.

- ## What happens when one partner in a couple gets sick?

When Jim's lover of two years, Paul, was diagnosed with AIDS, a few of his relatives asked him if he was going to stay with Paul or leave him. "I was floored," said Jim. "If my brother's wife had got sick two years after they got married, they never would have asked him that question. How could they think I would abandon him?"

There are people, of course, heterosexual and homosexual, who abandon sick spouses, but these cases are by far the exception. Far more typical is the story of Paulene and Helen. Paulene was first diagnosed with breast cancer in the mid-1970s and has been through a succession of surgeries and rounds of chemo- and hormone therapy. Helen is as devoted to Paulene as anyone could possibly be, making certain she's taking her medication, accompanying her to treatments, and offering more love and support than anyone could hope for.

▪ Can a gay spouse get medical benefits?

A handful of private companies and colleges, as well as a few local governments, offer the same benefits—including medical insurance—to the spouses of gay and lesbian employees as they offer to heterosexual married couples. (For more information on this subject, see chapter 7, "Work.")

▪ What's it like when a sibling gets married?

For many gay and lesbian people, a heterosexual sibling's marriage is often a reminder that no matter how comfortable they are being gay or lesbian, they are still different, and that no matter how accepting their parents are of their homosexuality, their couple relationship is not likely to be celebrated with nearly as much enthusiasm as that of a heterosexual sibling.

Gay and lesbian people who haven't yet told their families that they're gay can have an especially hard time. For Anita, her older sister's wedding meant having to answer the question, "So when are you getting married?" every two minutes for five hours. "But that wasn't the worst," said Anita. "When it came time to throw the bouquet, I hid in the bathroom. A search party came looking for me and dragged me back into the ballroom. My sister threw the bouquet right at me, so I had to catch it. What else could I do?"

Anita's family didn't know that her best friend, with whom she'd been sharing an apartment since graduating from college a couple of years earlier, was her lover of three years. Anita added, "Somehow I doubt my parents will want to give me the same kind of wedding they gave my sister when they know the whole story. I can't imagine my family accepting me, let alone announcing to the whole world that their daughter is marrying another woman. Can you imagine the wedding invitations? It makes me so angry on so many levels, including the fact I'll never have a full set of china!"

For gay and lesbian people who have told their families that they're gay, the wedding of a sibling can still cause all kinds of conflicts and mixed emotions. For example, when Ken's brother got married, the invitation to the wedding did not include Ted, Ken's partner of four years. "I was furious, but I didn't tell my brother how angry I was," said Ken. "I wasn't even sure at first if I was going to say anything, but Ted is *my* family, so I insisted that he be invited. But that wasn't the end of it. Then I had to figure out how to introduce Ted to my relatives, most of whom didn't know I was gay. I was sweating before we even got to the church."

▪ Do gay people marry straight people? Why?

Many, many gay and lesbian people marry heterosexual people, and for a variety of reasons.

Some gay and lesbian people marry heterosexuals because getting married is what we all learn is the right thing to do. Our culture is geared toward heterosexual married relationships, and gay people, like heterosexual people, want to fit in and "do the right thing."

Some gay and lesbian people who marry partners of the opposite sex do so with the hope that they'll "get over" their homosexual feelings. That was exactly what Edward hoped when he married Susanne. "We were both very young," said Edward, "and neither of us knew much of anything about homosexuality. I even told Susanne that I had had these feelings, but the psychiatrist I was seeing reassured us I would get over it, and

the best thing I could do was get married and have children."
Shortly after the birth of their second daughter, six years into
their marriage, and after ten years of seeing the same psychiatrist, Edward left his wife. "I didn't get over it. In fact, by the
time I left my wife—and fired my psychiatrist—I couldn't have
been more certain that I was gay and that my psychiatrist was
a quack."

Edward's experience is not uncommon. Plenty of psychiatrists and psychologists believed—and some still believe—that
homosexuality is something that can be, and should be, cured.
(See chapter 1, "The Basics" for more on this subject.)

Some gay and lesbian people enter heterosexual marriages
for cover, hoping to fulfill family or professional expectations.
Some don't inform their opposite-sex spouses beforehand.
Some do, and these include a number of closeted gay and lesbian celebrities, who have made arrangements—financial and
otherwise—with opposite-sex spouses to enter marriage.

Sometimes gay people marry heterosexual people for love,
friendship, and companionship. Sometimes the gay spouse in-
forms the heterosexual spouse prior to marriage and other
times not. I've known a few mixed gay male–heterosexual female couples in which the wives knew prior to marriage that
their husbands were gay, including one marriage that has
lasted for more than two decades.

Many gay and lesbian people at the time they marry a heterosexual spouse are either in denial about their sexuality or
are simply not fully aware of their sexual feelings. When Katie
married at the age of eighteen, she knew she "felt different
from other girls, but I didn't know why. It wasn't until I'd been
married for seven years and had four children that I had my
first adult crush on a woman. And would you believe it was a
woman in the church choir? Even after Mary and I became sexually involved, it still took me another year to admit to myself
that I was a lesbian. I couldn't even say the word!"

■ How do straight spouses react when they find out a spouse is gay?

According to Amity Pierce Buxton, author of *The Other Side of the Closet*, a book about the coming-out crisis for heterosexual spouses of gay and lesbian people, heterosexual spouses greet the disclosure as a denial of the relationship. "Shocked spouses," she writes, "typically feel rejected sexually and bereft of the mates that they thought they had. . . . Although relieved to know the reason behind changes in their partner's behavior or problems in marital sex, most feel hurt, angry and helpless." And though their homosexual spouses most often feel relief stepping out of the closet, and are likely to receive support from other gay and lesbian people, the heterosexual spouses suddenly find themselves in a closet of their own, fearful of telling anyone the truth about their gay or lesbian spouse.

■ Do any of these marriages last after a spouse finds out?

According to Buxton, "Although a number of couples succeed in preserving the marriage, the majority do not. Despite sincere efforts, the sexual disparity, competition for the partner's attention or unconventional—and for some, immoral—arrangements eventually become intolerable for most spouses."

■ What should you do if you think your spouse is lesbian or gay?

Before you do anything, find help. Find a friend you can talk to or a counselor who has experience dealing with your circumstances. Depending upon where you live, you may be able to find a support group for heterosexual people who have—or have had—gay or lesbian spouses. And you should also read *The Other Side of the Closet*, which is listed in the bibliography at the back of this book.

■ Do gay men and lesbians ever marry each other for "marriages of convenience"?

Yes, there are gay men and lesbians who have married and even had children together in order to appear heterosexual. Some people do it because of their careers, others because of family pressures. I remember one young woman in college who came from a very prominent and wealthy family. From what she knew about her parents, she assumed that they would never let her take over the family business if they discovered she was a lesbian, so she set out to find and marry a gay man with a similar need to appear heterosexual.

I should also add that there are gay and lesbian people who marry each other unknowingly and discover during the course of their marriage that both are homosexual.

■ Why do gay people hold hands in public?

Some gay people who hold hands in public do so to make a political statement, to make the point that gay people should be allowed to do the same things in public that heterosexual people do. But most gay people who hold hands in public do so for the very same reasons that heterosexual people do: they simply want to hold the hand of someone they care about. But because of public hostility toward gay and lesbian people, particularly those who display any kind of affection in public for a same-sex partner, they rarely hold hands in public without first considering where they are and whether or not holding hands would be a safe thing to do.

One friend, who enjoys holding her lover's hand in public, had a more blunt answer: "We hold hands because we're too scared to kiss and get shot." Sadly, this is not much of an exaggeration. Two gay men I know were attacked in midtown Manhattan in the middle of the day by a group of teenagers who spotted them holding hands as they crossed the street. One of the two suffered a fractured skull.

▪ How do gay and lesbian couples split up?

Gay and lesbian couples end their relationships in the same ways heterosexual couples do. It's just as painful, just as complex, and often just as ugly. But there *are* differences. Because gay and lesbian people can't get legally married, they can't get legally divorced. This may sound appealing at first— no divorce papers to file—but consider what can go wrong when there is money and/or property to be divided and no legal guidelines to follow.

When children are involved, money and property problems may seem insignificant by comparison. For almost all gay and lesbian couples who have children, only one partner is the legal parent. This is because a second parent can rarely adopt a child that already has a parent of the same sex (see chapter 4, "Family and Children," for more on this subject). In the event of a breakup, the nonadoptive second parent has no legal rights to even visit a child she or he may have raised since birth.

7

WORK

- ### Are there professions that attract large numbers of gay people?

Gay and lesbian people work in every profession, from the military to the arts, and do all kinds of jobs, from building roads to educating children. There are, however, certain professions and jobs that appear to attract a large number of gay or lesbian people. For example, it seems that more than the expected 10 percent of male nurses, male flight attendants, as well as male dancers and figure skaters are gay. And it seems that more than the expected 10 percent of female athletes, gym teachers, and military personnel are lesbians.

I've heard all kinds of possible explanations for this apparent phenomenon. I don't think any one explanation is adequate to explain why gay and lesbian people are represented in greater numbers in some jobs and professions, but in the absence of any concrete answers, some of the explanations I've heard are worth considering. One theory is that traditionally female professions attract gay men and traditionally male professions attract lesbians because gay men and lesbians are more likely to feel comfortable about crossing gender lines. Another is that gay and lesbian people are attracted to fields that have typically overlooked or been accepting of homosexuality, like the arts. One common stereotype is that gay men are attracted to certain jobs because more gay men than heterosexual men are artistically gifted, and that lesbians are attracted to certain jobs because more lesbians than heterosexual women are mechanically gifted. Indeed, some gay men are artistically inclined and some lesbians are mechanically inclined, but there is currently no scientific evidence to support the suggestion that gay men are any more artistically inclined than straight men and that lesbians are any more mechanically gifted than straight women.

Of the many explanations I've heard, I think it's easiest to understand how fear of discovery has led gay and lesbian people to pursue certain jobs or professions and avoid others. Journalist and writer Frank Browning noted, "In the past, once you realized that you'd been sentenced to a homosexual life, you assumed that a lot of worlds were closed to you because of the social expectations. There are forms of social performance that you're expected to meet, such as having a spouse and bringing a spouse to social functions. For this reason, many gay and lesbian people retreated into their own professional worlds and became florists or dog groomers or whatever. They pursued jobs and careers they could control, where they wouldn't be subject to someone else's judgment." Frank acknowledges that this is only a partial answer to a question that still remains to be adequately addressed.

- ## Are gay people more likely to pursue artistic careers?

It appears that gay men, at least, are more likely to pursue artistic careers than are heterosexual men. The AIDS crisis has made this tragically clear with a disproportionately high number of deaths from AIDS among the ranks of male dancers, actors, figure skaters, musicians, designers, and other artistic professionals.

- ## Are all male hairdressers, child care workers, elementary schoolteachers, decorators, and dancers gay?

- ## Are all female professional athletes, gym teachers, and military personnel lesbians?

No, but lots of gay men are hairdressers, child care workers, elementary schoolteachers, decorators, and dancers. And lots of lesbians are professional athletes, gym teachers, and military personnel. Whether or not gay and lesbian people indeed fill a larger percentage of jobs in these professions as opposed to all other professions won't be known for certain until gay and lesbian people can be accurately surveyed. If it's found that gay and lesbian people do fill a larger percentage of these jobs, then we still need an answer to why this is the case.

I should add here that because gay and lesbian people work in every profession, you can't assume that all men who work in what we think of as typically male jobs, like truck drivers, are heterosexual. Similarly, not all women who work in what we think of as typically female jobs, like child care workers, are heterosexual. And, of course, there are plenty of heterosexual male flight attendants, dancers, and florists, and plenty of heterosexual female gym teachers and athletes.

▪ Should gay people be allowed to be teachers?

Yes, and gay and lesbian teachers are already teaching in classrooms all across the country.

Those who object to gay and lesbian teachers in the classroom base their arguments on the mistaken twin assumptions that gay and lesbian teachers are more likely to molest their students than heterosexual teachers and that gay and lesbian teachers will set the wrong example and influence their students to become homosexuals.

First, the most likely person to molest children is a heterosexual male. His most likely victim is a female child. (For more on the subject of child molesting, see chapter 1, "The Basics," and the question "Are gay and lesbian people more likely to molest children?") Second, no one, not a teacher, a parent, or a favorite aunt can influence anyone to "become" a homosexual. You can't "make" a homosexual. You are, or you aren't. The best a gay or lesbian teacher can do is set an example as a positive role model to all children that you can be a gay or lesbian person *and* a good teacher. Plenty of us, including this writer, would have welcomed some positive gay and lesbian role models as we struggled through school in isolation.

I like what a lesbian comedienne once said about this point: "If teachers had that kind of influence over students, we'd all be nuns." The distinction here, of course, is that you *can* convince children to become nuns or priests. You *cannot*, however, convince anyone to become gay or lesbian. You can only encourage children to be who and what they already are.

▪ Should an openly gay teacher be allowed to teach?

This is an interesting distinction. Some people believe it's okay for gay and lesbian people to teach as long as they stay in the closet—in other words, hide the truth about who they are. As one antigay activist recently said to me, "It's okay as long as they leave their homosexuality at the front door."

Think for a second what it would mean for any teacher to leave his or her sexuality at the door. For a heterosexual teacher that would mean not wearing a wedding band to class, because the wedding band is a symbol of a heterosexual relationship. It would also mean that a heterosexual teacher could not bring a spouse to school social events. And it also means that if a student asked a personal question—for example, "Are you married?"—a married teacher would have to say, "I can't talk about my personal life," or would have to lie and say no.

Teachers are human, so inevitably their personal lives come up in class, particularly when students reach an age—junior high school, according to several teachers I spoke with—when they start asking teachers personal questions. Imagine what it's like for a gay or lesbian teacher when students ask, "Miss Shapiro, do you have a boyfriend?" "Are you married?" "How come we saw you on television in the Gay Pride march?" "Are you a lesbian?" A teacher who has to hide her homosexuality could not address any of these questions in an open and honest manner. And it goes beyond questions. "What am I supposed to do when students call each other *fag* and *dyke?*" said Miss Shapiro, who teaches high school outside Denver. "Am I supposed to sit there and let them use words like that? Should I challenge them, and tell them that saying *fag* and *dyke* is just as bad as saying *nigger* and *kike?* But then, because I'm defending gay people, my students might figure out that I'm a lesbian. And if they figure out I'm a lesbian, and someone complains to the administration, I could lose my job. Put yourself in my shoes. Would you want to live like that?"

- ## Are there companies that specifically welcome gay people?
- ## Are there companies that provide benefits to gay couples?

Yes. Increasingly, major corporations, including AT & T, IBM, Disney, and Citicorp, are making an effort to welcome gay and lesbian people. Xerox and Levi Strauss, for example, have policies prohibiting discrimination on the basis of sexual orientation. AT & T has sponsored an internal Gay Awareness Week. At other major corporations, gay and lesbian employees have organized their own groups. And due in large part to the research and lobbying efforts of these groups, a handful of companies, including Lotus Development Corporation, have extended the same benefits to the spouses of gay and lesbian employees that are offered to heterosexual spouses.

Also, of course, gay and lesbian social service agencies and organizations, as well as gay and lesbian owned and run businesses welcome gay and lesbian employees.

- ## What happens when gay and lesbian people come out at work or are found out?

Gay and lesbian people who come out of the closet at work or are found out have a range of experiences, from complete acceptance to being fired.

When Ralph was interviewing for his first job out of law school, he decided that he didn't want his sexuality to become an issue after he was hired. So before he was made an offer at the firm where he had worked the previous summer, Ralph had a talk with the hiring partner. "If there was going to be a problem, I wanted to know in advance so I could look for a job elsewhere. I walked into the hiring partner's office and asked him if

I could close the door. I told him I sensed there was a good chance they would offer me a job, and that they should know something about my personal life before they hired me, that I was gay. He asked me why I thought it was important to tell him that. I told him I didn't want it to come out later and then be a problem. He looked at me and said that was just his problem. He was gay and had always kept it a secret." Ralph was offered the job, and he accepted it.

When Carolyn first accepted her job as a Christian educator in the heart of a low-income housing community in Atlanta, no one asked her about her sexuality. But three years after she was hired, she was called into her boss's office and told that a student who stayed in her home had come across some things that indicated she was a lesbian. "Their biggest accusation was that I wrote checks to a gay church and that this girl saw pictures of me in my photo album sitting on the hood of my car with my roommate, with my arms draped around her. My boss asked if I was a lesbian, and I said that he didn't have the right to ask me that. Then he said, 'If you can't tell us that you're not, we need your resignation.' I said, 'When do you want it?' It was clear to me that there was no changing his mind."

Not everyone is either accepted or fired. Billie, a schoolteacher in a city near San Francisco, knows she won't be fired if her principal finds out that she's a lesbian, in part because her city forbids discrimination based on sexual orientation. "But I know they'll make my life so miserable that I'll have to quit. I hate living like this, but my partner is unemployed, and I can't afford to lose my job. So there's no way I would come out, and I'm doing everything I can to make sure no one finds out."

■ Why do people want to be openly gay at work?

See chapter 3, "Coming Out."

▪ Do some people want or *have* to stay in the closet at work?

There are plenty of people who are perfectly comfortable being in the closet at work and have no desire to share anything about their personal lives with their colleagues. Whether they have to keep their homosexuality a secret or not, they do.

There are also plenty of people who *have* to stay in the closet if they want to keep or succeed in their jobs or continue in their profession. For example, if you're a famous Hollywood actress, you could forget about playing any leading lady roles—or any roles, perhaps—if it were known publicly that you were a lesbian. Or if you work for a company that has a reputation for easing out suspected gay people, it would be in your interest to keep your homosexuality hidden or find another job. (For more on this subject, see chapter 3, "Coming Out.")

▪ Can you be fired from your job for being gay or lesbian?

Absolutely. In most places—with the exception of the more than one hundred municipalities and several states that forbid discrimination based on sexual orientation—it is perfectly legal to fire someone simply because he or she is gay. One of the more notorious cases in recent history involved Cracker Barrel Old Country Store, Inc., a restaurant and gift-store chain with more than a hundred outlets. In 1991, the company stated that it would no longer employ people "whose sexual preferences fail to demonstrate normal heterosexual values which have been the foundation of families in our society" and proceeded to fire all of its identifiable gay and lesbian employees, including valued long-term employees. Because federal civil rights legislation does not include protection of people based on sexual orientation and none of the states or localities where Cracker Barrel operates have civil rights laws that protect gay and lesbian people from job discrimination, the fired employees had no recourse except to look for new jobs. Cracker Barrel has since acknowledged its antigay policy, but says that it has now been rescinded, although the gay and lesbian employees who were fired say they have not been reinstated (as of early 1993).

Cracker Barrel is just one very obvious example, but sadly there are many such stories of gay and lesbian people losing their jobs simply because they are homosexuals, whether they work for the FBI, a major corporation, or the corner pharmacy.

■ Can you be openly gay and succeed professionally?

Not long ago, almost all gay and lesbian people had to hide their sexual orientation from their colleagues and employers for fear of being fired. But now, there is a growing number of examples of successful gay men and lesbians in a variety of professions who are open about who they are. There are, however, exceptions. It seems unlikely that openly gay military personnel will thrive professionally, even after President Clinton lifts the ban on gays in the military (which he has said he will do in July 1993). Only a tiny handful of professional athletes and high-profile actors are openly gay. And at the highest levels of corporate America you'll have a hard time finding anyone who is openly gay or lesbian.

■ Do gay and lesbian people bring same-sex spouses or same-sex dates to office parties?

Lots of gay and lesbian people wish they could bring their spouses or a same-sex date to company parties, but for several reasons very few do. To bring a same-sex date, you would have to be out of the closet at your job. To be out at your job, you would have to work at a company where gay and lesbian people are accepted. And even then, unless you worked for a company where most of the employees were gay, you would have to have enough courage and self-confidence to be one of the few (or the only) same-sex couples at the party. Also, your same-sex spouse or date would have to be comfortable with the idea.

One of the first times I went with a spouse to an office event, I remember being very nervous. I was afraid. I didn't know what to expect. His colleagues knew he was gay, as did his boss, but I was nervous and not all that sure I wanted to go. It turned out that the only problem was me. We were the only gay couple, but no one stared. No one pointed. In fact, everyone was very friendly. I wound up hanging out for most of the evening with the husband of one of the company's female executives. We even joked about being corporate spouses and weren't sure if we should be exchanging recipes or talking football, which neither of us knew anything about.

8

THE MILITARY

- ## What is the government's official position on gay and lesbian people in the military?

The service of openly gay and lesbian people in the military was the most contentious social issue tackled in the early days of the Clinton presidency. As of this writing (early 1993), the President has announced his plan to sign an executive order in July 1993 to lift the ban on gay and lesbian people in the military. Until that time, in an agreement worked out with congressional Democrats and the Joint Chiefs of Staff, new recruits will no longer be asked if they are homosexual, homosexuality will no longer be grounds for outright discharge from the military, and court proceedings against those discharged for being homosexual will be delayed. But service members who are gay remain subject to discharge proceedings and can still be removed from active duty. And those who have reached the point of discharge will be transferred to standby reserve, where they will receive no pay and no benefits.

- ## What are the reasons the military has given for excluding gay men and lesbians from serving in the military?

People in the military have over the years offered a long and changing list of reasons why gay and lesbian people shouldn't be permitted to serve in the military. Some of those who have opposed allowing gay people to serve once argued that gay men and lesbians were security risks because they could be easily blackmailed by someone threatening to reveal their secret life. But even the secretary of defense during the Bush administration dismissed that assertion, calling it "an old chestnut."

General Colin Powell, the chairman of the Joint Chiefs of Staff, who has strongly opposed the lifting of the ban against gay men and lesbians, has stated on a number of occasions that "the presence of homosexuals in the force would be detrimental to good order and discipline, for a variety of reasons, principally relating around the issue of privacy." Others have said that the presence of gay people would seriously impair the accomplishment of military missions by undermining the discipline, morale, and cohesiveness among the troops. Still others, including Commander Craig Quigley, a Navy spokesman, have said that if homosexuals are allowed to openly declare their sexual orientation, heterosexuals who shower with gay men would have an "uncomfortable feeling of someone watching." Quigley also noted, without offering any evidence, that homosexuals "are notoriously promiscuous."

But what of the hundreds of thousands of gay men and lesbians who have served in the military in the past and the many thousands who serve today? Military leaders have acknowledged the fact that gay men and lesbians have served and continue to serve alongside their heterosexual colleagues with apparently little difficulty. But, they argue, this is only because gay and lesbian people have been forced to hide their sexual orientation. As long as gay people are officially excluded, the argument goes, gay men and lesbians already in the military will not be a significant problem because they will have to behave themselves in order to keep their secret or risk being found out and discharged.

Since 1943, when the military first began officially excluding homosexuals, between 80,000 and 100,000 gay men and lesbians have been ousted from the military. According to the General Accounting Office, the annual cost of finding, discharging, and replacing homosexuals in the military is at least $27 million. And that figure does not take into account the human price—the thousands of ruined careers and lives.

▪ Do gay people make good soldiers?

Two reports commissioned by the Pentagon and released in 1989 concluded that there was no evidence that homosexuals were any greater security risk than heterosexuals and that they were no more likely to be subject to blackmail. One of the reports also found no evidence that homosexuals disrupted the armed forces, praised the performance of gay men and lesbians in the military, and urged their retention.

In 1990, the *New York Times* published a remarkable story that sharply highlighted the conflict between the Pentagon's official policy and the proven abilities of gay and lesbian service people. As reported, the commander of the navy's surface Atlantic fleet told his officers that homosexual women must be vigorously rooted out of the service. The commander warned in his instructions that investigations may be "pursued half-heartedly" by officers because lesbian sailors are generally "hardworking, career-oriented, willing to put in long hours on the job and among the command's top performers."

During the war with Iraq, the Pentagon apparently decided that gay and lesbian people were perfectly well qualified to serve. More than a dozen gay and lesbian reservists across the country were cleared by their unit commanders to serve in the Persian Gulf after stating their sexual orientation. But these reservists, who made quite clear that they wanted to serve, were also told that they would be discharged from the military once they returned from the war.

▪ What has the military done when it suspected a soldier was lesbian or gay?

According to a *New York Times* article reported by Jane Gross, those under suspicion of homosexuality have been interrogated and "suffer bright lights in their eyes and handcuffs at their wrists, warnings that their parents will be informed or their hometown newspapers called, threats that their stripes will be torn off and they will be pushed through the gates of the base before a jeering crowd. Further, those who have been interrogated said they were told that someone else had already identified them and so they might as well talk. They said they were promised an easier time if they would also supply investigators with information about others—first names, maybe, or a tip about a certain ship with a large gay contingent. Several people who have children said they had been threatened with loss of custody. A few reported verbal and physical abuse."

Journalist Randy Shilts, who documents the experiences of gay people in the military in his new book, *Conduct Unbecoming: Gays and Lesbians in the U.S. Military,* found examples of gay men and lesbians under investigation who were threatened with jail terms, as well as dishonorable discharges and the loss of military benefits, unless they turned over the names of other gay men and lesbians.

▪ What argument has President Clinton made for lifting the ban on gays in the military?

In making his case for lifting the military's ban on gay and lesbian people, Bill Clinton has said, "The principle behind this for me is that Americans who are willing to conform to the requirements of conduct within the military services in my judgment should be able to serve in the military, and that people should be disqualified from serving in the military based on something they do, not based on who they are. That is the elemental principle."

The President has also cited two reports to support his position. One study, by former President Bush's defense secretary, Richard Cheney, noted that gay and lesbian people who served in the military did so with distinction.

▪ Why do gay people want to be in the military?

In today's all-volunteer military, gay and lesbian people join for all the same reasons that heterosexual people do: pay, training, educational benefits, camaraderie, overseas travel, leadership challenges, and often a patriotic desire to serve their country. Some gay and lesbian people in the military also say they want to prove you can be gay in the Marine Corps, for example, and still be successful.

▪ Why did gay people join the military knowing they could be discharged?

Many of the gay and lesbian people currently in the military joined at a time in their lives when they were still either uncertain about their sexual orientation or were in deep denial about their homosexual feelings. Others knew they were gay or lesbian but saw the same career opportunities, or had the same desire to serve, as their heterosexual counterparts and gambled that they could keep their sexual orientation a secret.

- ## When did gay people first begin challenging the military's ban on gays?

Gay rights activists first challenged the U.S. military's ban on gay and lesbian people in 1964, when a handful of protesters picketed the Whitehall Induction Center in New York City, demanding that homosexuals be allowed to enlist. In 1975, Sergeant Leonard Matlovich and Ensign Copy Berg, both of whom were being discharged because they were gay, brought the first two lawsuits against the military in a bid to retain their jobs and overturn the military's antigay policy.

Many cases have been brought since, including the challenge made by Petty Officer Keith Meinhold, who was discharged in 1992 after stating on national television that he was a homosexual. His case was decided in January 1993 by a federal judge in California who ruled that the military ban on homosexuals is unconstitutional. The judge, Terry J. Hatter, Jr., permanently enjoined the military services from discharging or denying enlistment to gay people "in the absence of sexual conduct which interferes with the military mission." He then ordered the Navy to reinstate Keith Meinhold permanently. In his order Judge Hatter wrote: "Gays and lesbians have served and continue to serve the United States military with honor, pride, dignity, and loyalty. The Department of Defense's justifications for its policy banning gays and lesbians from military service are based on cultural myths and false stereotypes. These justifications are baseless and very similar to the reason offered to keep the military racially segregated in the 1940s."

- ## How have gay people managed to stay in the military?

Most gay and lesbian people have managed to stay in the military by carefully guarding their secret. A thirty-one-year-old officer at the Miramar Naval Air Station in San Diego, who guarded his secret for eight years, said in a 1990 *New York Times* interview, "This is not a life you'd choose for your worst enemy, but gays are very good at camouflage. Society puts us in that role from the first moment we discover our sexuality."

Sometimes the camouflage has included marrying a gay person of the opposite sex to give the appearance of a heterosexual marriage. Other gay and lesbian people have simply pretended to be straight, laughed at jokes about gay people, and have told stories about fictional heterosexual escapades when they had to.

Not all gay and lesbian people in the military remained completely hidden in the closet. Some were known as gay or lesbian to their colleagues and superior officers but were protected by them, at no small risk.

■ How do other countries handle the issue of gays in the military?

If President Clinton keeps his commitment to lift the ban on gay and lesbian people in the military, Great Britain will be the only one of the sixteen NATO countries to bar gay and lesbian people from military service. Most recently, Canada lifted its ban against gays and lesbians in October 1992, after a court ruled that its policy of exclusion violated the 1982 Canadian Charter of Rights and Freedom.

9

WHERE GAY AND LESBIAN PEOPLE LIVE

■ **Where do gay and lesbian people live?**

From watching television news reports, you might think that gay and lesbian people live only in New York, San Francisco, and Los Angeles. Not true. Gay and lesbian people live everywhere, from rural Kentucky to downtown Juneau, Alaska. It is true, however, that large numbers of gay and lesbian people migrate from rural areas and small towns and cities to large metropolitan areas.

■ **Why do gay and lesbian people move from smaller towns and cities to places like San Francisco and New York?**

Large cities in general have for many decades been magnets for gay and lesbian people in search of other people like themselves. San Francisco, New York, Chicago, and the nation's other major cities have long had significant gay and lesbian subcultures, including gay bars and restaurants. More recently, these cities have also developed significant gay and lesbian communities, complete with community centers, softball teams, choruses, and countless social, religious, and professional organizations. Also, large cities have traditionally provided the kind of anonymity that has allowed gay and lesbian people to keep their homosexual identities safely hidden, particularly from their families back home.

Although the major cities have long been popular with gay and lesbian people, it was World War II, according to historians John D'Emilio and Allan Berube, that led to the explosion of urban gay and lesbian subcultures. They explain that tens of millions of American men and women were uprooted during the war to serve in the military and to work in the war industries. Most of these men and women, including millions of gay and lesbian young people, moved to or traveled through the major industrial and port cities. It was in New York, Chicago, San Francisco, and other cities that these gay and lesbian people discovered for the first time that they weren't alone.

Following the war, rather than return to the small cities and towns they once called home, many gay and lesbian people chose to remain in the major cities.

■ How did San Francisco become such a popular place with gay and lesbian people?

One possible explanation for San Francisco's popularity among gay and lesbian people early on, besides its status as a major port city and its long-standing reputation for tolerating people who lead unconventional lives, was suggested to me by San Francisco Municipal Court Judge Herbert Donaldson.

As a young attorney, Herb Donaldson was involved with an early gay rights organization in San Francisco called the Society for Individual Rights. SIR, along with other gay and lesbian organizations in San Francisco, organized a fund-raising ball for the evening of January 1, 1965. The event turned into a major confrontation between the police, who didn't want the event to take place, and the hundreds of gay and lesbian people who attended. Several people were arrested, including Herb Donaldson.

According to Judge Donaldson, "The police made this estimate that there were seventy thousand homosexuals in the city. There weren't, but when they carry it on the wire services that there are seventy thousand, you've got seventy thousand others out in the country who want to come and join that seventy thousand here! They're still coming."

By the 1970s, San Francisco's large and politically active gay and lesbian population, in combination with the city's reputation as a relatively friendly place for gay men and lesbians and its mild climate and physical beauty, made it a popular destination for gay people in search of a better life.

■ Why do gay and lesbian people create their own neighborhoods in the major cities?

Some—not most—gay and lesbian people live in predominantly gay neighborhoods, and they do so for many of the same reasons people from different ethnic, racial, and religious groups often wind up segregated into their own neighborhoods: safety, comfort, community, a sense of feeling welcome, and discrimination.

It's no secret that gay and lesbian people are often targets of physical attacks. Living in a predominantly gay neighborhood offers the safety of knowing that your neighbor is unlikely to attack you for being gay. Unfortunately, these neighborhoods are also often destinations for teenagers looking for a gay person to attack.

Living in a community where there are lots of other gay and lesbian people or where gay and lesbian people make up the majority of residents is for many people more comfortable than living where they're the only gay people or couples in the neighborhood. For single people, a predominantly gay and lesbian neighborhood also offers more opportunities to meet and socialize with other gay and lesbian people.

In San Francisco's Castro neighborhood, many of the shopkeepers, as well as the doctors, dentists, tailors, and so forth, are gay or lesbian, or gay-friendly, so you can be yourself and not worry about being judged. You also don't have to worry about discrimination. For example, if you're looking for an apartment with your same-sex partner in a predominantly gay neighborhood, you aren't likely to encounter a landlord who doesn't rent to gay people or to gay and lesbian couples.

■ What are some gay neighborhoods, and what are they like?

Most major cities have neighborhoods that are popular with gay and lesbian people. For example, in Washington, D.C., the Dupont Circle neighborhood is popular with gay and lesbian people—as well as with young families and young single people. In Los Angeles, it's West Hollywood, which is actually an incorporated city. In New York City, it's Chelsea or the West Village. In Houston, it's the Montrose neighborhood.

Most city neighborhoods popular with gay and lesbian people look very much like any other neighborhood except that there are stores, restaurants, and bars that cater to a gay and lesbian clientele. You also might see more identifiably gay and lesbian people on the street. And occasionally you might see male couples and lesbian couples holding hands.

The first time I walked down Castro Street, the main commercial street of San Francisco's predominantly gay and lesbian neighborhood, I was a little uncomfortable. Even though I'm gay, I had never been on a public street where there were so many gay and lesbian people. That may sound funny, but it wasn't something I was used to. This was just before Gay Pride Day in 1980, so Castro Street was overflowing with gay and lesbian tourists.

For me, the most startling sight was the many same-sex couples holding hands. People were behaving so normally—in other words, not censoring their behavior for heterosexual public consumption—that at first it didn't seem normal to me. Years later, I'm still surprised to see two people of the same sex holding hands on the street, but rather than think of it as abnormal, I'm struck by the courage it takes to act normally in a world that is often so dangerous for people publicly identifiable as gay or lesbian.

▪ What is it like for gay people who live outside the major cities, in the suburbs, for example?

Gay men and lesbians, no matter where they live, have had all kinds of experiences, both positive and negative, with their heterosexual neighbors. For Connie and Renata, who decided to move from New York City to a suburban, almost rural, neighborhood in New Jersey, the experience was mixed. The two women, who had been a couple for nearly twenty years, didn't anticipate problems with their new neighbors, but they were a little apprehensive. "We thought we might have some problems, but we had our hopes up," said Connie.

One afternoon, a few months after they moved in, Connie and Renata found the word *dyke* spray-painted on their front door. "That scared us to death," said Renata, "but we decided to repaint the door and hope that it wouldn't happen again." It didn't, in part, they think, because they made a concerted effort to get to know their neighbors. "We hoped that once people got to know us, they'd treat us just like any other neighbors," said Connie.

Do they have any regrets? "No. This was something we wanted to do," said Renata. "We weren't twenty-five anymore, so we didn't care about nightlife. We just wanted peace and quiet and a backyard. That sounds hopelessly dull, but it's what we wanted. Maybe we should have done a better job of anticipating that not everyone would welcome us, but we've learned—and our neighbors have learned—from the experience."

10

SOCIALIZING AND FRIENDS

- ### Where do gay people meet?

Gay and lesbian people meet in all the places heterosexual people meet, from the grocery store, the office, and singles bars to professional organizations, social clubs, and computer bulletin boards. But, unless the singles bar or professional organization is specifically for gay and lesbian people, gay people must assume that almost everyone they meet is not gay.

- ### Why do gay and lesbian people go to bars and belong to organizations that are just for gay people?

When you're gay or lesbian, you are by definition an outsider: outside the norm, outside the mainstream, different. And no matter how well integrated you are into your community, college, profession, or family, you are still not a part of the majority.

When you enter a gay or lesbian bar or play on an all-gay softball team, you're no longer an outsider—you're normal. You can be yourself, which includes being physically affectionate in a way that heterosexual people take for granted. There's no fear of being judged or discriminated against for being gay. At its best, the experience is the sense of being with "family."

When I attended the first conference of the National Lesbian and Gay Journalists Association in San Francisco, the experience was extraordinary. More than three hundred gay and lesbian journalists attended, and while there was plenty of disagreement about all kinds of political and professional issues, it was remarkable to share experiences and ideas with gay and lesbian journalists from across the country and the professional spectrum. For many who attended, the conference was their first opportunity to talk with other gay and lesbian journalists.

I hasten to add that gay and lesbian people aren't one big happy family. Gay people are just as capable as anyone else of making all kinds of judgments, whether about race, age, looks, or the way you dress. For example, Craig, who is in his mid-twenties, thought he would feel welcome when he began socializing in the gay world. "What I quickly discovered," he said, "was that I was incredibly naive. When I walked into a bar—and that's assuming I could get in without having to show three types of identification—the first thing people saw was a black man, not just another gay man. You can't believe the stereotypes people hold onto. If I meet one more white man who thinks I'm some sort of sexual amazon just because I'm black, I'll scream. I thought gay people would know better—and some do—but more often than not, gay people and straight people treat me just the same."

▪ What is a gay bar like?

First, it's important to understand that gay and lesbian bars have historically played a key role in gay and lesbian social life because until fairly recently, bars were the only public places gay people could meet and socialize. Though that's often no longer the case, particularly in major cities, bars still play an important role.

There are all kinds of gay and lesbian bars. In big cities like New York, Chicago, and Los Angeles, different bars cater to different kinds of people. There are bars for men, women, older men, younger men; there are country and western bars, young professional bars, hustler bars, bars with back rooms (for those interested in sexual encounters), S & M bars, you name it. In smaller cities and towns, there may only be one bar for everyone. On a visit to Juneau, Alaska, several years ago, I went to that city's one gay and lesbian bar. It was at the back of a restaurant a few blocks from downtown. The bar itself was about six feet in length. There were eight stools and enough room for another four people to stand. You had to meet everyone in the bar, because there was no way not to. The bartender joked that the bar was only gay until someone straight walked in.

The first time I went to a gay bar, I was seventeen and very scared. I don't know what I thought went on in a bar, but to me the whole thing was mysterious, even exotic, but nonetheless terrifying. My friend Bob, who was my tour guide, told me what to expect, that it would be no different from a straight singles bar, except that there would be no women. I was too embarrassed to tell Bob I had never been in a straight singles bar.

We walked through the door; no one checked my ID, even though I was underage. The place was dimly lit, smoky, and very crowded. The music was too loud for real conversation, but people were talking. On the left, men were seated at the bar. Men were also standing along the walls and talking in groups. Most were casually dressed in jeans and pressed shirts. The average age was probably thirty. Lots of people were just standing around looking at each other and looking a little bored. We stayed for about half an hour and left. Looking back, I think what I feared most was the possibility that I would be attacked by the gay men at the bar, but no one even looked at me twice.

■ What kinds of social organizations do gay people have?

Gay and lesbian people have all kind of organizations, from gay and lesbian college fraternities and alumnae and alumni groups to square dancing and gardening clubs, computer user groups, and marching bands. A recent New York City events calendar listed the following predominantly gay and lesbian organizations (or organizations that hold meetings specifically for gay and lesbian people): ACT UP (AIDS Coalition to Unleash Power), Alcoholics Anonymous, American Gay Atheists, Art Anonymous, Asians and Friends of New York, Axios Eastern and Orthodox Christians, Big Apple Bodybuilding Association, BIGLYNY (Bisexual, Gay, and Lesbian Youth of New York), Bisexual S/M Discussion Group, Body Positive (support group of HIV-positive people), Bronx Lesbians United in Sisterhood, Business Owners' Support System, Butch/Femme Society, Christian Science Group, Club Frottage, The Coalition of Lesbian and Gay City Employees, Cocaine Anonymous, Couples Together, Debtors Anonymous, Dignity—Big Apple (social events and liturgies for gay and lesbian Catholics), Education in a Disabled Gay Environment, Fire-FLAG (Fire Fighters Lesbian and Gay of New York), Gay and Lesbian Alliance Against Defamation, Gay and Lesbian Anti-Violence Project, Gay and Lesbian Educators, Gay and Lesbian Independent Democrats, Gay and Lesbian Italians,

Gay and Lesbian Reading Group, Gay and Lesbian Social
Workers, Gay Artists Group, Gay Asian and Pacific Islander
Men of New York, Gay Fathers Forum, Gay Male S/M Ac-
tivists, Gay Men of African Descent, Gay Men Incest and Sex-
ual Abuse Survivors Anonymous, Gay Officers Action League,
Gay Pilots Association, Gay Veterans Association, Girth and
Mirth Club of New York, Herpes Support Group, Irish Gay and
Lesbian Organization, Israelis and Friends, Knights Wrestling
Club, Las Buenas Amigas, Latino Gay Men of New York,
Lavender Bytes, Lesbian and Gay Teachers, Lesbians in the
Creative Arts, Males Au Naturel, Men of All Colors Together,
Metro Gay Wrestling Alliance, Minority Task Force on AIDS,
Narcotics Anonymous, Natural History Group, New York
Advertising and Communications Network, New York Area
Bisexual Network, New York Bankers Group, OLGAD (Orga-
nization of Lesbian and Gay Architects and Designers), Other
Countries—Black Gay Men's Writing Workshop, Overeaters
Anonymous, Prime Timers, Professionals in Film/Video, Psy-
chology Discussion Group, Queer Nation, Queer Night Out,
Scrabble Players Club, Sex and Love Addicts Anonymous Les-
bians, Sexual Compulsives Anonymous, Sirens Motorcycle
Club, Social Activities for Lesbians, Society of Spankers,
Southern Asian Lesbian and Gay Association, Times Squares,
Twentysomething, Uncircumsized Society of America, Village
Dive Club, Village Playwrights, Waters of Life, Women Entre-
preneurs in Business, and the Women's Playwright Collective.
And this list doesn't include the Gay Men's Chorus, and Front
Runners, and . . .

▪ What do gay and lesbian people talk about when they get together?

In addition to talking about all the things that heterosexual
people talk about, many gay and lesbian people talk about being
gay and about the latest news on gay and lesbian rights issues.

An acquaintance once asked me why gay people made such a big deal about being gay and talked about it all the time. I explained that once being gay wasn't a big deal within our society and once our civil rights were no longer questioned, we would probably stop talking about it.

■ Why are there so many gay people in Provincetown?

Provincetown on Cape Cod is one of several resort areas popular with gay and lesbian people. Others include Palm Springs, California; Rehoboth Beach, Delaware; The Pines and Cherry Grove on Fire Island in New York; and Key West, Florida. These resorts offer hotels, restaurants, stores, and bars that cater to gay and lesbian people. Beyond the physical amenities, these resorts offer something no other resorts can offer gay people: lots of other gay and lesbian people. When you travel to one of these resort areas, you don't have to worry about being the only gay or lesbian people on the street or at the beach.

Of all these resorts, The Pines and Cherry Grove on Fire Island offer the "gayest" environment. Accessible only by ferry from the eastern end of Long Island, these two small summer communities are almost entirely populated by gay and lesbian people, which means you can feel entirely safe holding your sweetheart's hand in public and not draw a single stare.

■ What are gay and lesbian cruises?

These are exactly what they sound like: chartered cruise ships specifically for gay and/or lesbian people that sail to places near and far.

■ Do lesbians and gay men get along?

Historically, within the gay and lesbian rights movement, there have been tensions between lesbians and gay men, and often for good reason. In the early days, back in the 1950s, most gay men treated lesbians the way most heterosexual men treated women. "They thought we were there to serve coffee and donuts," said one activist, now in her seventies. But though there have always been tensions and often distance between the gay male and lesbian worlds, and despite the fact that plenty of lesbians have nothing to do with gay men and plenty of gay men have nothing to do with lesbians, there have also been many long-lasting friendships between lesbians and gay men. In addition, the AIDS crisis has led to many close ties between gay men and lesbians, as they've worked side-by-side caring for ill friends, and in AIDS professional and volunteer organizations.

▪ Do gay and lesbian people have heterosexual friends?

Plenty do. Some don't. But even for gay and lesbian people who have heterosexual friends, these friendships may fade over time. Of the many people I've spoken with about this issue, Ann Northrop's experience seems common. Ann never lost any straight friends when she told them she was a lesbian, but she drifted apart from them. "Your interests are not the same anymore," said Ann, "and sometimes it's because they're so egregiously stupid about lesbians that it's painful to be with them. And look, the fact is, when you're with gay friends, you're a whole person. That's not how I feel when I'm with my straight friends. I find it sad that it's not as easy now for me to socialize with or be with my straight friends, who I had all my life and who I love dearly. I think it's very sad, because I don't want my life to be limited that way. And I don't want to think of us all in our separate little communities. But I'm coming to the realization that we really are separate and that we really do like to be with people of our own kind, whether that's class or race or sexual orientation or gender."

▪ Do gay people lose straight friends when they come out of the closet?

It depends on the friends. Often friends can handle the news, but sometimes they can't. Nancy came out to her friends when she was in college. Most of her friends were supportive, but when Nancy told her best friend, "she got real distant. It's upsetting, and it still upsets me because we had been such good friends. It was such a catch-22 kind of thing, because I needed my friends most at that time, but I also feared my friends because I didn't know how they would react if they knew I was gay."

▪ Why do some heterosexual women have a lot of gay male friends? Isn't there a nickname for such women?

One woman who has many gay male *and* lesbian friends had this to say in an interview in the *Seattle Times:* "I really enjoy gay men because they don't try to put me in a mold. I enjoy my lesbian friends because they're very strong, interesting people. They don't see the limitations that other women see in their lives."

Nancy May, a heterosexual woman who was a gay rights activist in the 1960s, was often called names because she had a lot of gay male friends. "Sometimes I was called a 'fag hag' or a 'fruit fly.' When I first heard the expressions, I had to get them explained to me. A fruit fly is usually somebody who runs around with a hairdresser. A fag hag is somebody who just hangs out with gay men. Both terms sound real derogatory, but sometimes they were used in a real offhand, lighthearted, kidding kind of way."

▪ If you think a friend is gay, what should you say?

The standard answer to this question is to suggest that you say something that indicates you're sympathetic and supportive of gay and lesbian people—to let your friend know that it's okay to tell you that he or she is gay. For example, you could say, "Oh, you know, I saw this great thing on TV last night. It explained a lot to me, and I really loved it, and wasn't it nice to see a same-sex couple be so affectionate." The reasoning behind this suggestion is that you give your friend or loved one the opportunity to come out, to be honest about his or her sexual orientation, without having to directly ask the question, "Are you gay?"

Now, that's the standard answer, but this isn't the only way to approach a friend who you think is gay or lesbian. You can also be more direct—and you may need to be more direct, particularly if an indirect approach doesn't work—and say, "I feel really awkward talking to you about this, but you're my friend and I love you and I want to be able to have an honest relationship with you. I'm pretty sure that you're gay and I want to talk to you about that. Maybe I'm wrong, but I hope you'll tell me the truth."

If you're not comfortable talking directly to a friend about the fact that you think he or she is gay or lesbian, you can put your thoughts in print. For example, you could write, "For a long time I've wanted to talk to you about something, but I haven't been able to find a way to bring it up. My impression is that you're gay. I love you as my friend and want you to know that I'm completely comfortable with this . . . " and so on.

11

RELIGION

- **Is homosexuality a sin?**
- **Is homosexuality immoral?**

No, although not everyone will agree with me. Fortunately, we live in a nation where morality and religious beliefs are not legislated but are a matter of personal choice.

In recent years, these questions of whether or not homosexuality is immoral or sinful have been the subject of great debate. The result has been enormous conflict within the nation's mainstream religions and continuing heated discussion within American society. (For a survey of how a variety of religions view homosexuality, see "What do different religions say about gay men and lesbians?" later in this chapter.) The following thoughts are from just three of the many people who have offered definitive pro-gay responses to the questions of morality and sin.

Frank Kameny, who was fired from his job at the U.S. Army Map Service in 1957 because he was gay, first examined the morality question as part of his fight to get his job back. Frank pursued his case right up to the Supreme Court, and in preparing his petition to the Supreme Court in late 1960, he concluded that homosexuality was moral. "At that time, the government put its disqualification of gays under the rubric of immoral conduct, which I objected to. Because under our system, morality is a matter of personal opinion and individual belief on which any American citizen may hold any view he wishes and upon which the government has no power or authority to have any view at all. Besides which, in my view, homosexuality is not only *not* immoral, but is affirmatively moral. Up until that time nobody else ever said this—as far as I know—in any kind of a formal court pleading." The Supreme Court refused to hear Frank's case, and he later went on to form a pioneering gay rights organization in Washington, D.C. In part because of Frank's dogged efforts, the federal government officially stopped excluding homosexuals from government employment in 1975.

Carolyn Mobley, an assistant pastor for the Metropolitan Community Church, a Christian church whose membership is primarily gay and lesbian, at first believed her sexual orientation was sinful. But as a college student, she realized that her sexuality was not sinful but, instead, a gift from God. She credited the Rev. Martin Luther King, Jr., with helping her come to terms with being a lesbian. "Dr. King's commitment to disobeying unjust laws had a profound impact on my thinking. I began to question the things that I was told to do: 'Are they really right? Are they right if I'm told they're right by a person in a position of authority?' I began to realize that parents could steer you wrong. Teachers could steer you wrong. Preachers,

God knows, could steer you wrong. They were all fallible human beings. That really changed my way of looking at myself and the world. And it certainly helped me reevaluate the message I was getting from the church about homosexuality. It made me examine more closely what Scripture had to say about it.

"I continuously read Scripture on my own. I especially reread Romans numerous times. I finally got the picture that God wasn't against homosexuals, and that even Paul, who wrote that passage in Romans about homosexuality and was against homosexuals, was a human being subject to error, just like me. So I thought the man was wrong, period. What he was espousing was inaccurate, and it needed to be challenged. That was what Dr. King was about, challenging error wherever it was found.

"I continued to reinterpret that whole Romans scripture about giving up what was natural for something unnatural, and a light went off in my head. Paul had a point. His argument about doing what was natural really did make sense, but you had to know what was natural for you. It was unnatural for me to have sex with a man, so I decided that I wouldn't do that again. The only natural thing was for me to do what I'd been feeling since Day One in the world. Why would I try to change that? How foolish I'd been. I thought to myself, *Thank you, Paul. I got your message, brother. We're okay.*

"When that light went on in my head, I knew it was from God, that it was my deliverance. God didn't deliver me from my sexuality. God delivered me from guilt and shame and gave me a sense of pride and wholeness that I really needed. My sexuality was a gift from God, and so is everyone's sexuality, no matter how it's oriented. It's a gift to be able to love."

Episcopal Bishop John Shelby Spong, an outspoken supporter of the ordination of gay and lesbian people and the blessing of same-sex relationships, also believes that homosexuality is not a sin. He had the following to say when asked by Parents and Friends of Lesbians and Gays to answer the question, In your opinion, does God regard homosexuality as a sin?: "Some argue that since homosexual behavior is 'unnatural,' it is contrary to the order of creation. Behind this pronouncement are stereotypic definitions of masculinity and femininity that reflect the rigid gender categories of patriarchal society. There is nothing unnatural about any shared love, even between two of the same gender, if that experience calls both partners into a fuller state of being. Contemporary research is uncovering new facts that are producing rising conviction that homosexuality, far from being a sickness, sin, perversion, or unnatural act, is a healthy, natural, and affirming form of human sexuality for some people. Findings indicate that homosexuality is a given fact in the nature of a significant portion of people, and that it is unchangeable.

"Our prejudice rejects people or things outside our understanding. But the God of creation speaks and declares, 'I have looked out on *everything* I have made and "behold it [is] very good"' (Genesis 1:31). The word of God in Christ says that we are loved, valued, redeemed, and counted as precious no matter how we might be valued by a prejudiced world."

▪ What does the Bible say about gay men and lesbians?

The Bible really doesn't say all that much about sex between men and says absolutely nothing about sex between women. Among the Bible's 31,173 verses, there are less than a dozen verses that mention sexual acts between men.

I like what Peter J. Gomes, an American Baptist minister and professor of Christian morals at Harvard, had to say in a 1992 *New York Times* editorial regarding what is written in the

Bible about homosexuality: "Christians opposed to political and social equality for homosexuals nearly always appeal to the moral injunctions of the Bible, claiming that Scripture is very clear on the matter and citing verses that support their opinion. They accuse others of perverting and distorting texts contrary to their 'clear' meaning. They do not, however, necessarily see quite as clear a meaning in biblical passages on economic conduct, the burdens of wealth, and the sin of greed.

"Nine biblical citations are customarily invoked as relating to homosexuality. Four (Deuteronomy 23:17, I Kings 14:24, I Kings 22:46, and II Kings 23:7) simply forbid prostitution by men and women. Two others (Leviticus 18:19–23 and Leviticus 20:10–16) are part of what biblical scholars call the Holiness Code. The code explicitly bans homosexual acts. But it also prohibits eating raw meat, planting two different kinds of seed in the same field and wearing garments with two different kinds of yarn. Tattoos, adultery, and sexual intercourse during a woman's menstrual period are similarly outlawed.

"There is no mention of homosexuality in the four Gospels of the New Testament. The moral teachings of Jesus are not concerned with the subject.

"Three references from St. Paul are frequently cited (Romans 1:26–2:1, I Corinthians 6:9–11, and I Timothy 1:10). But St. Paul was concerned with homosexuality only because in Greco-Roman culture it represented a secular sensuality that was contrary to his Jewish-Christian spiritual idealism. He was against lust and sensuality in anyone, including heterosexuals. To say that homosexuality is bad because homosexuals are tempted to do morally doubtful things is to say that heterosexuality is bad because heterosexuals are likewise tempted. For St. Paul, anyone who puts his or her interest ahead of God's is condemned, a verdict that falls equally upon everyone.

"And lest we forget Sodom and Gomorrah, recall that the story is not about sexual perversion and homosexual practice.

It is about inhospitality, according to Luke 10:10–13, and failure to take care of the poor, according to Ezekiel 16:49–50: 'Behold, this was the iniquity of thy sister Sodom, pride, fullness of bread, and abundance of idleness was in her and in her daughters, neither did she strengthen the hand of the poor and needy.' To suggest that Sodom and Gomorrah is about homosexual sex is an analysis of about as much worth as suggesting that the story of Jonah and the whale is a treatise on fishing."

Peter Gomes goes on to say later in his editorial that "those who speak for the religious right do not speak for all American Christians, and the Bible is not theirs alone to interpret. The same Bible that the advocates of slavery used to protect their wicked self-interests is the Bible that inspired slaves to revolt and their liberators to action.

"The same Bible that the predecessors of [the Rev. Jerry] Falwell and [the Rev. Pat] Robertson used to keep white churches white is the source of the inspiration of the Rev. Martin Luther King, Jr., and the social reformation of the 1960s.

"The same Bible that antifeminists use to keep women silent in the churches is the Bible that preaches liberation to captives and says that in Christ there is neither male nor female, slave nor free.

"And the same Bible that on the basis of an archaic social code of ancient Israel and a tortured reading of Paul is used to condemn all homosexuals and homosexual behavior includes metaphors of redemption, renewal, inclusion and love—principles that invite homosexuals to accept their freedom and responsibility in Christ and demand that their fellow Christians accept them as well."

▪ What did Jesus have to say about homosexuals or homosexuality?

Nothing.

■ What do different religions say about gay men and lesbians?

The only thing the many different religions agree on about homosexuality is that they don't agree. That goes for different religions as well as different denominations within religions and different religious leaders within the same denomination. But for the sake of bringing a little order to the cacophony of discordant voices within the religious world, here's a general survey of what the major religions in the United States have to say on the subject, drawn, in part, from the *San Francisco Examiner*.

The United Methodists let openly gay people join and do not officially consider homosexuality a sin, but a special committee of the church has been unable to agree (as of late 1992) on the central question it was asked to resolve: whether homosexual activity is compatible with Christian belief.

The Mormon church does not let openly gay people join, considers homosexuality a sin, and recommends chastity for homosexuals. The Roman Catholic church permits openly gay people to join, considers homosexuality a sin if practiced, and teaches that any sexual activity outside marriage is wrong.

The Baptists officially let openly gay people join and consider homosexuality a sin, but the American Baptists and Southern Baptists differ in their views, and individual churches are autonomous. So although the Southern Baptist Convention may condemn homosexuality as "a manifestation of a depraved nature" and "a perversion of divine standards," one of its member churches, the Pullen Memorial Baptist Church in Raleigh, North Carolina, held a "blessing of holy union" for two gay men.

The Episcopal church lets openly gay people join, does not consider homosexuality a sin, and urges congregations to provide dialogues on human sexuality. One of the most outspoken supporters of gay and lesbian rights is Episcopal Bishop John Shelby Spong.

The Lutherans let openly gay people join, consider homosexuality a sin, and believe that it is not in God's original plan. Presbyterians don't have one voice on this issue except regarding the ordination of gay and lesbian people. The highest court of the Presbyterian church ruled in November 1992 that an openly gay, sexually active person cannot serve as a minister of any of its 11,500 churches; the ruling nullified the hiring of a lesbian as a co-pastor of a church in Rochester, New York.

Moslems do not let openly gay people join, consider homosexuality one of the worst sins, and encourage homosexuals to change. Orthodox Jews believe that homosexuality is an abomination, but on the other end of the Jewish spectrum, the Reform and Reconstructionist movements have established special outreach programs for gay people and have even accepted them publicly into their rabbinical associations. Covering the middle ground of Judaism is the Conservative movement, which has welcomed gay and lesbian people to its congregations but does not allow them to become rabbis.

The best news comes from the Buddhists, who welcome openly gay people, ordain them, don't consider it a sin, and have no formal teaching policy on gay and lesbian people. Hallelujah!

▪ Why is there so much antagonism between the Catholic church and gay and lesbian people?

The Catholic church has been extremely harsh in its condemnations of gay and lesbian people and often actively opposes the rights of gay and lesbian people.

In 1990, the National Conference of Catholic Bishops approved a document on human sexuality that labeled homosexual behavior evil but said that gay people themselves were not sinful. Commenting on the document at the time it was approved, Bishop Edward O'Donnell of St. Louis said, "The tendency or the orientation is a disorder, but the person is not an evil person."

Beyond this official "love the sinner, hate the sin" policy toward homosexuals, what has most infuriated gay and lesbian people and gay and lesbian rights supporters has been the insistent opposition of the Catholic church to gay and lesbian equal rights, as well as its opposition to AIDS prevention education that involves any mention of condoms.

The most recent example of official antigay church policy came in June 1992 in the form of a Vatican memo to the leaders of the 57 million Roman Catholics in the United States. The document reiterated the church's position that homosexuality is an "objective disorder" and maintained that for the sake of the "common good," U.S. bishops should oppose legislation barring discrimination against homosexuals in areas that include adoptions, placement of children in foster care, military service, and employment of teachers and athletic coaches.

▪ Who are some prominent antigay religious leaders?

Among the best-known antigay religious leaders are the Rev. Lou Sheldon, who runs the Anaheim-based Traditional Values Coalition; the Rev. Pat Robertson, a former presidential candidate, whose Christian Coalition has vigorously opposed gay rights efforts; and the Rev. Jerry Falwell, who wrote in a 1991 letter to followers describing his "national battle plan" to fight gay rights, "We surely love their souls. But we must awaken to their wicked agenda for America!"

▪ Has organized religion always opposed homosexuals?

According to historian John Boswell, in his 1980 book *Christianity, Social Tolerance, and Homosexuality*, up until the end of the twelfth century, Christian moral theology treated homosexuality "as, at worst, comparable to heterosexual fornication but more often remained silent on the issue." But then, on the heels of a diatribe from Saint Thomas Aquinas, the church began to view homosexuals as both unnatural and dangerous.

■ Are there organizations and places of worship specifically for gay people who are religious?

There are organizations all across the country specifically for gay and lesbian people who are Catholic, Jewish, Episcopal, Lutheran—you name it. Also, most major cities have a gay and lesbian synagogue. In addition, the Metropolitan Community Church, whose membership is primary gay and lesbian, has more than 250 congregations in the United States and around the world. (In late 1992, the National Council of Churches, the nation's largest ecumenical organization, voted against giving observer status to the Universal Fellowship of Metropolitan Community Churches.)

■ Can openly gay people become ministers and rabbis?

More and more openly gay and lesbian people are being ordained as ministers and rabbis, but the entire issue of their ordination has led to heated debates and bitter conflicts across the religious spectrum. For example, while the Episcopal church doesn't officially endorse ordination of openly gay and lesbian people, local bishops are free to ordain homosexual clergy if they wish—and they've done so.

The Conservative movement of Judaism rejected a proposal in March 1992 that would have allowed gay people to serve as rabbis in the movement's eight hundred synagogues. But at the same time, the nation's largest gay synagogue voted overwhelmingly to hire a lesbian rabbi. Because the synagogue, which has many Conservative members, isn't affiliated with the Conservative movement, it wasn't subject to its ruling.

■ How have religious institutions and clergy been involved in the gay rights effort?

Some oppose gay rights. But some religious institutions and clergy have been very actively involved in supporting the rights of gay and lesbian people. For example, in 1965, a group of liberal ministers, along with local gay rights activists, staged the first major public gay and lesbian fund-raising event in San Francisco for a new organization called the Council on Religion and the Homosexual. More recently, in 1992, several mainstream religious groups, including the National Council of Jewish Women (Portland Section), joined in the successful effort to defeat an anti–gay rights statewide ballot initiative in Oregon.

■ Can you become heterosexual through prayer?

Prayer may do a lot of things, but one thing it won't do is make a homosexual into a heterosexual.

It may seem harmless to suggest that prayer is the answer to becoming a heterosexual, but as Mary Griffith, who once held Christian fundamentalist beliefs, discovered, it can be deadly. Mary believed that if her teenaged gay son, Bobby, prayed hard enough, he would become heterosexual.

Bobby prayed, all the while fearing he would be punished by God for his homosexuality. He wrote in his diary, "Why did you do this to me, God? Am I going to hell? That's the gnawing question that's always drilling little holes in the back of my mind. Please don't send me to hell. I'm really not that bad, am I? I want to be good. I want to amount to something. I need your seal of approval. If I had that, I would be happy. Life is so cruel and unfair." A year and a half later, at the age of twenty, Bobby jumped off a highway overpass and landed in the path of an eighteen-wheel truck.

In a letter to other gay young people printed in the *San Francisco Examiner*, Mary Griffith later wrote, "I firmly believe—though I did not, back then—that my son Bobby's suicide is the end result of homophobia and ignorance within most Protestant and Catholic churches, and consequently within society, our public schools, our own family.

"Bobby was not drunk, nor did he use drugs. It's just that we could never accept him for who he was—a gay person.

"We hoped God would heal him of being gay. According to God's word, as we were led to understand it, Bobby had to repent or God would damn him to hell and eternal punishment. Blindly, I accepted the idea that it is God's nature to torment and intimidate us.

"That I ever accepted—*believed*—such depravity of God toward my son or any human being has caused me much remorse and shame. What a travesty of God's love, for children to grow up believing themselves to be evil, with only a slight inclination toward goodness and that they will remain undeserving of God's love from birth to death.

"Looking back, I realize how depraved it was to instill false guilt in an innocent child's conscience, causing a distorted image of life, God and self, leaving little if any feeling of personal worth.

"Had I viewed my son's life with a pure heart, I would have recognized him as a tender spirit in God's eyes."

12

DISCRIMINATION AND ANTIGAY VIOLENCE

■ How are gay people discriminated against?

Gay and lesbian people are discriminated against in many different ways. People have, for example, been fired from their jobs, evicted from their homes, and denied custody of their children. Until recently, gay and lesbian people were routinely discharged from the military. (For more on this subject, see chapter 8, "The Military.") In nearly half the states, gay and lesbian people can be arrested for having sex with another consenting adult in the privacy of their own homes. Gay student groups have been refused official recognition by universities. Gay and lesbian people have been thrown out of fraternities and sororities. Gay boys are not permitted to join the Boy

Scouts. Gay and lesbian couples are also not permitted to legally marry, and gay people have even been denied service in restaurants.

In a high-profile discrimination case in Los Angeles in the early 1980s, a lesbian couple made a reservation at a restaurant that had special booths for romantic dining. The restaurant refused to serve them, because the manager claimed the booths were reserved for "mixed" couples. The two women brought a discrimination lawsuit against the restaurant and eventually won their case, but rather than serve same-sex couples, the restaurant owner removed the restaurant's romantic dining booths.

Discrimination is not usually nearly so obvious as being refused service at a restaurant or receiving a pink slip or an eviction notice. More typical is a landlord who won't rent to two "single" men (only married couples) or a job promotion that never materializes.

■ How are gay and lesbian people harassed?

Harassment of gay and lesbian people ranges from name-calling and spray-painting antigay epithets on the homes of gay and lesbian people to slashing tires on cars parked outside gay bars and vandalizing offices of gay and lesbian organizations. But all too often, antigay incidents go well beyond name-calling to death threats, beatings, and even murder.

■ Is antigay violence a new problem or a big problem?

Talk to older gay and lesbian people and you quickly discover that antigay violence is nothing new. Barbara Gittings, an early gay rights activist, recalled an incident in the 1950s at a gay bar in New York City: "I was with my friend Pinky. I don't remember why we called him Pinky, but anyway, Pinky got friendly with a couple of uniformed guys who had come into the bar, Marines, I believe. They were sitting and talking with us. When the four of us left the bar, out came the brass knuckles. They proceeded to rip up Pinky's face. They cut open his nose entirely. And they said to me, 'We aren't touching you, Sonny, because you wear glasses.' It was terrifying, and there was not a damn thing I could do until they had finished their dirty work and left. Then I helped Pinky up and got him to a hospital. He had thirteen stitches in his nose. I guess in my innocence I hadn't thought people could be so hateful and violent toward us. Pinky didn't want to report it to the police. He figured they wouldn't do anything about it and they might give him a hard time. He was probably right."

Several early gay rights activists I spoke with talked about how they couldn't call the police after incidents like the one Barbara Gittings described, because, they said, the police were often the ones who did the beating.

Today, the issue of antigay violence is being taken more seriously by public authorities. A number of government reports have concluded that gay and lesbian people are the most frequent victims of hate-motivated violence. Following the passage of the National Hate Crimes Statistics Act in 1990, the federal government began collecting statistics from sixteen thousand police departments on crimes motivated by prejudice, including prejudice based on sexual orientation. How many victims? The total number of reported antigay attacks in five of the nation's major metropolitan areas in 1991 was 1,822, a 31 percent increase over 1990; eight people were killed. But many of those who monitor these numbers agree that only a small percentage of the victims of antigay attacks report these incidents, because people fear that their sexual orientation will be made public or that their reports won't be taken seriously by the police, or because they fear being abused by the police.

- ## How do the police combat antigay violence?

As police departments have begun to take antigay violence more seriously, a handful have launched decoy programs to catch "gay-bashers"—people who physically attack gay men and lesbians. For example, in Houston, Texas, police walked the streets of a downtown neighborhood where gay-bashing had been a problem dressed as potential victims. Within hours after the first decoys took to the streets, two officers posing as a gay couple were sprayed with Mace, and two days later another undercover officer was beaten with a baseball bat.

- ## What have gay and lesbian people done to combat antigay violence?

In several cities that have neighborhoods with large numbers of gay and lesbian residents, gay men and women have organized street patrols to try to stop antigay attacks. For example, in July 1990, a group called the Pink Panthers began patrolling the streets of the West Village in New York City between midnight and three in the morning on Fridays and Saturdays. The Pink Angels in Chicago, who work closely with that city's police, patrol the predominantly gay and lesbian section of Chicago's North Side. Both San Francisco and Houston have similar patrol groups.

- ## Why do people discriminate against, harass, and attack gay men and lesbians?

Some do so because they believe that homosexuality is sinful and immoral or that homosexuals are child molesters, disease carriers, and/or mentally ill. Others believe that homosexuality is contrary to American family values and threatens to destroy the American family. For years, the U.S. military has claimed that gay people were security risks, a threat to morale, and "prejudicial to good order and discipline."

University of California research psychologist Dr. Gregory M. Herek, author of *Hate Crimes: Confronting Violence Against Lesbians and Gay Men*, states that for most people who are biased against gay people, homosexuals "stand as a proxy for all that is evil . . . such people see hating gay men and lesbians as a litmus test for being a moral person."

Other psychologists who have studied antigay bias say it results from a combination of fear and self-righteousness in which gay people are perceived as contemptible threats to the moral universe. Experts also agree that these antigay feelings are often supported by religious institutions that consider homosexuality to be sinful.

There are still other reasons people discriminate against, verbally harass, and physically express their hate for gay men and lesbians. Young people in particular are often motivated by a desire to be a "part of the crowd" or to gain the approval of their peers or family. Another often-heard explanation for what motivates people who are antigay is fear of their own homosexual feelings. According to Dr. Herek, "Although the explanation probably is used more often than is appropriate, it does apply to some men who will attack gays as a way of denying unacceptable aspects of their own personalities."

When Jean, who describes herself as "not exactly a Marilyn Monroe type," was beaten up several years ago, her attackers made perfectly clear what they didn't like about her. "These four guys were yelling antilesbian remarks: 'Who do you think you are? You wanna look like a man? We'll show you!' That kind of stuff." Jean was walking home from the gym in New York's Greenwich Village. "There was a woman with them, but she didn't say that much. They came up behind me and started kicking a tin can at me. By the time I got to the end of the block, they were kicking it pretty hard, and it was hitting me. So I turned around. I remember saying something like,

'What's the matter here?' And the guy hit me. His first punch broke my nose. The other person hit me in the stomach. I couldn't stand up after that. I fell down. I was already a bloody mess, and then one of them kicked me in the back." Jean suffered permanent damage to her spine.

13

SEX

No discussion of sex can begin without addressing the issue of AIDS and the importance of practicing safe sex—doing what's necessary to prevent the spread of HIV, the virus that causes AIDS. For questions on AIDS, see chapter 18, "AIDS." And for the latest information on safe sex and how to prevent infection with HIV, talk to your doctor, call a local health organization or local or national AIDS information hotline. The National AIDS Hotline, at 1-800-342-AIDS, is staffed around the clock by information specialists who can answer your questions about AIDS and HIV.

- ### What do they do?
- ### How do gay and lesbian people have sex?

First, what do we mean by "having sex"? A heterosexual young man who asked me what gay people consider "having sex" told me that for him having sex meant intercourse with a woman. Everything else was "just fooling around." I like using a broader definition. For the purpose of this question, sex means stimulating each other sexually. And let's not forget the emotional component, because for many people, sex means both physical and emotional intimacy.

There's no mystery about what gay and lesbian people do to stimulate each other sexually, because what gay and lesbian people do is essentially what heterosexual people do. Generally, people do what makes them feel good. That means looking at each other, talking to each other, kissing, holding hands, massaging each other, holding each other, licking each other, in short, stimulating each other in some way that makes them feel aroused. Of course, some things feel better than others, because some parts of the body are naturally more sensitive, like nipples, breasts, buttocks, the clitoris, the penis, the anus, lips, and for some people, that tender spot on the back of the neck. People use all kinds of things to stimulate the parts that feel good, including fingers, hands, the tongue, the mouth, the penis, toes—you name it, people use it.

Having sex may or may not include reaching orgasm. And just as there are all kinds of ways to stimulate each other sexually—oral, manual, and so on—there are all kinds of ways to reach orgasm, although reaching orgasm usually requires stimulating the penis (for men) and stimulating the clitoris and/or the G-spot (for women).

■ What about intercourse?

(It's important to note that sexual intercourse—both anal and vaginal—without the use of a condom offers the highest risk of contracting AIDS. So before engaging in sexual intercourse or any other sexual activity with another person, please learn what you need to know about safe sex and preventing infection with HIV.)

Two men can, if they choose, have anal intercourse—insertion of the penis of one man into the anus of the other. Some men achieve orgasm in this way.

Two women who desire vaginal penetration can use fingers, toes, a dildo, or whatever feels good to them. Some lesbians who desire the experience of intercourse use a dildo attached to a waist harness that allows one woman to have intercourse with another.

■ How can a lesbian be sexually fulfilled/ satisfied (i.e., achieve orgasm) without a penis during intercourse?

Any woman—heterosexual or homosexual—can tell you that you don't need a penis to achieve an orgasm, and that penile-vaginal intercourse does not guarantee an orgasm. What is usually required to achieve orgasm is stimulation of the clitoris, which is located outside and above the vagina, and/or the G-spot, which is located inside the vagina. The clitoris can be stimulated using a number of different things, including fingers, the mouth, or a vibrator. And if a woman desires vaginal stimulation, a penis isn't required, because there are many different ways to penetrate and stimulate the vagina without a penis. These include using fingers, tongues, dildos, and so forth.

■ Do all gay men regularly engage in anal intercourse?

No, this is a myth. However, some people—gay and straight, men and women—find anal stimulation and/or penetration with a penis, fingers, dildo, or whatever, pleasurable. Others don't. And some men—gay and straight—enjoy inserting their penis into the anus of a partner—male or female. Others don't.

I know this seems like a very short answer to what for many people is a very highly charged issue, but whether or not two people choose to have anal intercourse or one partner stimulates another partner's anus or wants to have his or her anus stimulated is really just a matter of personal preference.

■ Why do some gay men have anal intercourse while others don't?

Gay men who engage in anal intercourse do so because it gives them pleasure, gives their partner pleasure, or both.

Gay men who don't engage in anal intercourse, either as the one doing the penetrating or the one being penetrated, give a number of different reasons. I remember one of my gay friends commenting on this topic when someone asked him if he had ever "been screwed by another man." His answer: "I can't get anything out, let alone, in!" My friend explained that he had had both chronic severe constipation and hemorrhoids since his mid-teens and that having intercourse with a man was the last thing he wanted to do to his body.

So some gay men find it physically uncomfortable to be anally penetrated by a penis. Other men find it uncomfortable, either because they don't want to assume what is considered a traditionally passive role or because of the social taboo regarding anal sex. Others fear the possibility of contracting AIDS, even with the use of a condom (see chapter 18, "AIDS," for more information on this topic). And for others still, anal intercourse is now too closely associated with AIDS and death to be any source of pleasure.

■ Do lesbians use sex toys?

■ Do gay men use sex toys?

Ask any purveyor of sex toys about who buys and uses the various sexual implements available, and you'll find out that all kinds of people, male and female, gay and straight, old and young, use sex toys.

▪ Do gay men use pornography?
▪ Do lesbians use pornography?

Some do, some don't. But glancing at the shelves of any store that sells pornographic magazines and sells or rents videotapes, it's easy to see that there's a much larger market for pornography that appeals to gay men than for pornography that appeals to lesbians. And just the same, there is a much larger market for pornography that appeals to straight men than there is for pornography that appeals to straight women.

▪ If a lesbian uses a dildo, doesn't that imply she wants to be with a man?

No. A lesbian who uses a dildo is simply choosing this type of vaginal or anal stimulation—just as when a heterosexual man uses a dildo for anal stimulation it doesn't mean he wants to have intercourse with a man.

▪ What are tops and bottoms?

Years ago, I was having a conversation with an acquaintance, and he casually mentioned, "Well, as a top . . ." I stopped him mid-sentence and asked him what he was talking about. He explained that a "top" was the one who always penetrated during anal intercourse, and a "bottom" was the one who was always penetrated. (He didn't exactly use the same words I'm using here.)

The distinction between "tops" and "bottoms" is also made among some lesbians, where a "top" always uses a dildo or other implement to penetrate a "bottom."

Some people also use the "top" and "bottom" labels for whoever takes the aggressive versus the passive role when having sex of any kind. Though some gay men and lesbians strictly define their sexual roles as "tops" or "bottoms," others do not use these labels and are likely to shift from more aggressive to less aggressive roles from minute to minute, hour to hour, day to day, week to week.

■ Is a lesbian's clitoris bigger than that of a heterosexual woman?

The size of a woman's clitoris is not dependent on her sexual orientation.

■ Do gay men have bigger sexual appetites than straight men?

The popular myth is that gay men have enormous sexual appetites and have sex all the time. The truth is dull to report. Gay men and straight men are different only in who they desire, not how much they desire.

■ Are lesbians virgins?

■ What, for gay men, is considered losing your virginity?

This question reminds me of a conversation I had with a woman friend in college. Long after she told me about all the fun she'd been having with her new boyfriend, she said that she intended to remain a virgin until she married. Boy, was I perplexed! I thought back over our earlier conversations about how her boyfriend had done this to her or how she had done that to him. There was plenty of talk about what I thought sounded like passionate, sweaty, messy, lusty sex. How, I asked her, could she define herself as a virgin after all that sex? "I've never had intercourse," she explained. Oh. After thinking about it, I had to agree that my friend was technically a virgin, but only because she had never had a penis in her vagina. By her own description his penis had been almost everywhere else.

Using the penile penetration definition of virginity doesn't work quite so well for gay men and lesbians. For example, is a sexually active lesbian who has never had intercourse with a man still a virgin? Is a sexually active gay man who has never been penetrated anally by another man still a virgin? What if he has penetrated another man but never been penetrated himself?

Given the realities of sexual relations between men and women, men and men, and women and women, I think it's time for a new definition for virginity. So I vote for the definition that says you are no longer a virgin if you've had sexual relations with another person involving genital stimulation to orgasm.

▪ Do gay people in relationships have less sex over time?

Just like heterosexual couples, most gay and lesbian couples have less sex with each other over time.

▪ Do gay people feel guilty about having sex with each other?

Okay, okay, I admit it. When I was a young man I felt very guilty about having sex with men. By the time I became sexually active, I knew I wanted men, but I also knew that according to everything I had learned, homosexuality was wrong, so of course I felt guilty about doing something wrong. But my guilt was nothing compared to the story one man told me about a relationship he had with a man who was devoutly

Catholic. "Every time after we had sex, barely a second after my boyfriend had an orgasm, he would be out of bed, on his knees, genuflecting and begging God for forgiveness. I can't believe I managed to put up with that for six months before breaking up with him. He needed help, and I tried, but there was nothing I could do for him."

My experience and that of the devout Catholic is not everyone's experience. The first time Sonya had sex with another woman, she didn't feel guilty at all. "Making love to a woman felt like the most perfectly natural thing in the world for me. I was thirty-two. This is what I wanted. I'd waited all my life for it. Why in heaven's name would I feel guilty? I felt like going out and celebrating!"

- ## Can a gay person have sex with someone of the opposite sex?
- ## Is it pleasurable?

Most gay and lesbian people have had sex with someone of the opposite sex. That should come as no surprise, given that that's what we all learned we were supposed to do. And though sex with the opposite sex may not have been our first choice, for many gay and lesbian people there was still pleasure in the experience.

- ## Are gay men physically repulsed by women?
- ## Are lesbians physically repulsed by men?

Just because you have sexual feelings for people of the same sex, you aren't necessarily physically repulsed by the opposite sex. Most gay and lesbian people simply don't have significant sexual feelings for the opposite sex.

When I first came out to some of my straight male friends in college, a couple of them assumed I found women physically repulsive. I explained how I felt by telling them a story about my girlfriend in summer camp when I was in my early teens. Eva had brown hair, green eyes, and a nice body. She was pretty, fun, and adventuresome. We had a great time together. We even held hands and liked to cuddle. But when the other boys talked about trying to get to first or second base with their girlfriends (this was twenty years ago, and none of us even considered the possibility of getting to home base), I remember thinking that I'd rather play cards. If the other boys hadn't mentioned it, the possibility of getting sexual with Eva never would have occurred to me, but I certainly wasn't repulsed by her.

■ Are gay men promiscuous? Why?

If you believe what some people say about gay men, you would think that all gay men have had a thousand or more sexual partners by the time they're thirty. Some very sexually active men—straight and gay—have had a thousand or more sexual partners by the time they're thirty, but most single gay men feel lucky if they can get a date on Saturday night.

Most gay men who have lots of different sexual partners aren't doing it because of a desire to challenge society's general condemnation of promiscuity. They're doing it for a simple reason: they want to.

■ What are gay bathhouses and sex clubs?
■ Why do gay men go?
■ Do women go to these kinds of places?

Gay male bathhouses and sex clubs are actually two different things. A gay bathhouse is typically set up like a health club and may have a weight room, a TV room, a sauna, a steam room, a swimming pool, and other amenities. There may also be cubicles with beds that you can rent. When you enter a bathhouse you're assigned a locker where you put your clothes.

The reason gay men go to bathhouses is generally to have sex, not lift weights. So once your clothes are in your locker, the search for a sexual partner or partners begins. There is no lesbian equivalent of gay male bathhouses.

Sex clubs, which have become very popular in recent years, are designed to appeal to all kinds of people and often don't have a permanent location. In other words, a sex club event may be held at one location this week and another the next week. Some sex clubs are strictly for gay men, some for lesbians, some for both, some for heterosexual people, some for those into S & M, and so forth. In major cities, if you have a sexual desire, you can usually find a sex club where you can satisfy it, no matter what your sexual orientation.

■ Why do gay men have sex in bathrooms and public parks?

Historically, public parks and rest rooms were just about the only places besides gay bars where men could find other men for sexual encounters. And though public parks and rest rooms meant risking arrest by undercover police, they allowed for even greater anonymity than did gay bars. At a time when almost all gay people kept their homosexuality a secret, anonymity was paramount.

Though gay men can now find sexual partners in lots of other places, some continue to seek out and engage in sex in public places. Men who do this give several different reasons for engaging in public sex. Some men find this kind of sexual encounter convenient and quick. As one man explained, "There's no negotiating. You don't have to buy anyone a drink. You don't have to figure out whose home you're going to go to. You don't even have to say a single word." Other men find the sense of danger inherent in public sex to be sexually exciting. Others like watching other men engage in sex. And still others want the anonymity of public sex because they're in a married heterosexual relationship, deeply closeted, or involved in a couple relationship with another man.

▪ Do lesbians engage in sex in public rest rooms and public parks?

In general, lesbians do not engage in public sex. But, all kinds of people—straight and gay, men and women—at one time or another have had sex in public parks, rest rooms, airplanes, on beaches, and so on.

14

MASS MEDIA

- **Has Hollywood portrayed gay people accurately?**
- **Why do gay people protest movies that portray gay men and lesbians in a negative way?**

Gay and lesbian people—individually, through organized protests, and through the Gay and Lesbian Alliance Against Defamation—have complained plenty about how they've been portrayed by Hollywood, and with good reason. Almost without exception, gay and lesbian people are portrayed in mainstream Hollywood movies as murderers, twisted villains, victims, or wimps. It's difficult to get through a movie without someone making an antigay joke or using offensive words like *fag* or *dyke*. And though gay people don't feel compelled to kill themselves on screen as often as they once did, they still blow out their brains every now and then. All this is thoroughly documented by the late film historian Vito Russo in his book *The Celluloid Closet: Homosexuality in the Movies.*

When I've been asked this question in the past and offered the above answer, people usually note that Hollywood has portrayed every ethnic, racial, religious, or other kind of group in a negative way at one time or another. True, but Hollywood movies have also portrayed these people in positive ways as well, so at least there's some balance. When it comes to gay and lesbian people, there is rarely any attempt to portray them in a realistic and balanced manner.

▪ But aren't there some movies that portray gay and lesbian people positively?

Yes, some, including *Desert Hearts, Parting Glances,* and *My Beautiful Laundrette,* but almost without exception, movies like these have been produced independently.

▪ Has television portrayed gay people accurately?

Not long ago, I caught an episode of "Lost in Space," a 1960s television show I watched religiously when I was a kid. I was stunned to realize as an adult that one of the show's main characters, Dr. Smith, was clearly played as a stereotypically gay man. He was effeminate, timid, and physically weak. But that wasn't all. He was also duplicitous, scheming, selfish, and downright evil. Week after week he put the lives of the other characters at risk as he sought to enrich himself, fill his stomach, or find his way back to Earth. Not exactly a fine role model.

In recent years, network television shows have done a lot better than "Lost in Space" in presenting a range of gay and lesbian characters, but gay men are still rarely seen on television, and lesbians, even more rarely. When gay men and women do appear on the little screen, their homosexuality is usually treated as a "special issue" or the story is about gay men and

AIDS. Gay men and women are almost never simply absorbed into a script without fuss. One striking exception is "Rosanne," which has had both a recurring gay male character and, more recently, a recurring lesbian character played by comedienne Sandra Bernhard.

■ Why do advertisers object to gay characters or themes on TV?

Advertisers traditionally avoid being associated with any controversial topic, particularly homosexuality. They fear turning off potential customers and don't want to invite the wrath of antigay activists through product boycotts, for example. Because of this fear, advertisers sometimes pull their sponsorship of shows they object to. For example, in 1991, shortly before "Thirtysomething," a popular television show about a group of friends in their thirties, aired an episode that showed two gay men in bed (they were just talking), advertisers withdrew their sponsorship, costing the network that broadcast the show big bucks. But curiously, a 1991 episode of "L.A. Law" that claimed to show network television's first lesbian kiss lost no advertisers. Homosexuality between women seems not to disturb advertisers as much as homosexuality between two men does.

■ Why do gay people have their own magazines and newspapers?

■ When were the first magazines published by gay people?

■ What did newspapers and magazines say about gay people in the 1950s and 1960s and earlier?

Gay and lesbian publications offer two things that mass market, mainstream publications can't. First, they provide gay and lesbian readers with the kind of in-depth news and information they want about issues that concern them and aren't

likely to find anywhere else. Second, they serve advertisers trying to reach a gay and lesbian market.

When the first gay and lesbian magazines were published in
the 1950s, they were just about the only places where gay and
lesbian people could read anything about themselves that
didn't include such headlines as "Nest of Perverts Raided,"
"How L.A. Handles Its 150,000 Perverts," "Great Civilizations
Plagued by Deviates," and "Pervert Colony Uncovered in
Simpson Slaying Probe." (These are actual newspaper headlines from mainstream newspapers in the mid-1950s.) But
most often, gay and lesbian people were simply ignored.

Though stories on gay and lesbian people appeared with in-
creasing frequency in the mainstream press through the 1960s
and 1970s, most of the coverage was biased against gay people.
One of my favorite examples comes from an unsigned essay in
the January 21, 1966, issue of *Time* magazine. The essay, entitled "The Homosexual in America," stated, "For many a
woman with a busy or absent husband, the presentable homosexual is in demand as an escort—witty, pretty, catty, and no
problem to keep at arm's length. . . . The once widespread view
that homosexuality is caused by heredity, or some derange-
ment of hormones, has been generally discarded. The consen-
sus is that it is caused psychically, through a disabling fear of
the opposite sex." The essay noted that both male and female
homosexuality were "essentially a case of arrested development, a failure of learning, a refusal to accept the full responsi-
bilities of life. This is no more apparent than in the pathetic
pseudo marriages in which many homosexuals act out conventional roles—wearing wedding rings, calling themselves 'he'
and 'she.' " The essayist saved the best for last: "[Homosexual-
ity] is a pathetic little second-rate substitute for reality, a
pitiable flight from life. As such it deserves fairness, compas-
sion, understanding and when possible, treatment. But it
deserves no encouragement, no glamorization, no rationaliza-

tion, no fake status as minority martyrdom, no sophistry about simple differences in taste—and above all, no pretense that it is anything but a pernicious sickness."

Today, many mainstream publications are doing a better job of accurately reporting major gay and lesbian stories, but no matter how good they get, mass market newspapers and magazines can't offer what special-market publications can.

■ Are there a lot of books published just for gay and lesbian people?

Back in 1988 I was on a national tour following the publication of my first book, *The Male Couple's Guide.* My sister and brother-in-law came to my book signing at Lambda Rising, a large gay and lesbian bookstore on Connecticut Avenue in Washington, D.C. I thought I had told them what kind of a bookstore it was, but apparently I hadn't. As my sister chatted with the store manager, my brother-in-law wandered off to look around the store, which looks just like any other independently owned bookstore. At the same moment I heard my sister say, "You mean *all* the books here are gay books?" my brother-in-law wandered back, wide-eyed. He said he had no idea that you could fill an entire store with books for gay and lesbian people. Lambda Rising stocks more than six thousand titles that are of specific interest to gay and lesbian readers.

Gay and lesbian publishing has become big business as the industry has discovered what independent gay and lesbian publishers have known for a long time—gay and lesbian people read just like everyone else and, in fact, buy more books than the average reader.

The first bookstore specifically for gay and lesbian people, the Oscar Wilde Memorial Bookshop, opened in 1967 in New York City's Greenwich Village. Today there are dozens of such stores across the country, and many major bookstores also have special gay and lesbian sections.

15

SPORTS

- ### Why don't gay men like sports?

Okay, okay, I admit it. I don't like competitive sports and couldn't care less which baseball or football team is in first place. So I should have known I was gay after the tenth time I struck out playing baseball in summer camp, right? But what about one of my gay male friends, who flies from city to city to follow his favorite football team and is an avid triathlete? And how do you explain the thousands of gay men who participate in the Gay Games (see "What are the Gay Games?" later in this chapter), not to mention the many closeted gay male professional athletes?

The fact is, lots of men are good at and/or like sports, and that includes lots of gay men. And plenty of men are bad at and/or don't like sports, and that includes plenty of heterosexual men. Are gay men more likely to be bad at and/or dislike sports than heterosexual men? I doubt it, but until someone figures out a way to survey the largely invisible and hidden gay population, we won't know the answer for sure.

▪ Are all women athletes and women physical education teachers lesbians?

One of the classic stereotypes about lesbians is that all lesbians are good athletes. Indeed, there are women athletes and physical education teachers who are lesbians, but there are also plenty of lesbians like my friend Linda, who can't throw a ball or swing a golf club to save her life. And, of course, there are plenty of women athletes and physical education teachers who are heterosexual.

According to Dr. Dee Mosbacher, a psychiatrist who is producing a video on homophobia and women in sports, the question isn't how many lesbian women are in sports, but why some people are playing into the public's fear of homosexuality and accusing women in sports of being lesbians. "The charge of lesbianism," explained Dr. Mosbacher, "is used for several reasons. For example, when recruiting women athletes for college, some coaches have tried to attract certain women by suggesting that the coach at a competing school is a lesbian. And the charge of lesbianism has also been used to discourage or avoid hiring female coaches. As women's sports have become significantly more lucrative in recent years, and more men have been competing for coaching jobs, we've seen an increase in this kind of accusation against women coaches."

▪ What are the Gay Games?

The first International Gay Athletic Games was held from August 29 through September 5, 1982, in San Francisco. More than 1,300 athletes from fifteen countries participated.

The 1994 Gay Games will be held in New York City. More than 15,000 athletes from forty countries are expected to participate.

The Gay Games was originally named the Gay Olympics, but the U.S. Olympic Committee, which by act of Congress owns the word *Olympic*, brought a lawsuit prior to the first Gay Games and succeeded in preventing the event's organizers from using the word. And this was despite the fact there had been many other legally unquestioned "Olympics" for all kinds of things, including Olympics for dogs, frogs, and hamburger chefs.

The purpose of the Gay Games, according to a Gay Games spokesperson, is to "hold a true Olympic event, open to all participants, whose goal is to do their personal best. The event is sponsored by the lesbian and gay community to celebrate lesbians and gay men and promote our self-esteem, pride, and dignity."

The Gay Games was founded by Dr. Tom Waddell, a 1968 U.S. Olympic decathlete. (Waddell also helped organize the famous protest by black U.S. athletes at the 1968 Mexico Summer Olympics.) He died from AIDS in 1987.

▪ Are there any openly gay star athletes?

Very few professional athletes, star or otherwise, have come out of the closet during or after their careers. The list of professional athletes who have come out is short and includes tennis superstar Martina Navratilova, former San Francisco 49er running back Dave Kopay, former Oakland A's outfielder Glenn Burke, former Mr. America and Mr. Universe Bob Jackson-Paris, and swimmer Bruce Hayes, who won a gold medal at the 1984 Summer Olympics in the 800-meter freestyle relay and seven gold medals at the 1990 Gay Games.

■ Why aren't there more?

Professional athletes fear risking their careers, as well as lucrative product endorsements, should their homosexuality become public knowledge. And their fears are not unfounded. Former 49er Dave Kopay couldn't get any job in football after he came out publicly in 1975. Kopay had hoped to coach on the college level, but he couldn't find anyone willing to hire him at any level, so he went to work at his uncle's floor covering store in Hollywood.

Even for a seemingly untouchable high-profile star like tennis great Martina Navratilova, there is a price to pay for being honest. Besides being accused by former tennis champion Margaret Court of ruining the sport and setting a bad example for younger players, Navratilova has said in interviews that being open about her sexual orientation has led to her receiving fewer offers for product endorsements.

16

EDUCATION

- **What do students learn about homosexuality in school (elementary school through high school)?**

Students learn plenty about homosexuality in school, almost all of it informally and nearly all of it bad. The first lesson is when one child calls another a *fag* in the elementary school cafeteria, and the lessons continue right on through high school, when a group of students decides to torment a theater teacher they think is gay.

Formal education about homosexuality is more remarkable for what isn't said than for what is said, because with few exceptions, almost nothing is said. School curricula are virtually devoid of gay subjects. The more than forty year history of the gay rights movement doesn't come up in social studies lessons that include discussions about women's rights or black civil rights. Historical and contemporary figures—authors, artists, politicians, and so on—who are gay are rarely if ever identified as such. And high school books almost never even mention the words *homosexual, lesbian,* or *gay.*

Now, about the exceptions, which are, thankfully, growing in number. Some high schools have begun to educate their students on the subject of homosexuality. For example, in Fairfax County, Virginia, public high school students are shown a short film called, "What If I'm Gay?" Other high school districts, including several suburban school districts in the Chicago area, invite gay and lesbian organizations to send speakers to talk about homosexuality, to help alienated—and hidden—gay and lesbian students feel less alienated, and to teach students about AIDS. When Ann Northrop visited New York City high schools to speak about homosexuality, her goal was not to debate gay politics. "I didn't have arguments with them about issues like gay marriage. I talked to them about feelings, and I talked to them about sex, and I talked to them about relationships, and I let them ask all the real questions they had."

Sometimes the students asked very real and very blunt questions. Once, following a class at a junior high school, one twelve-year-old boy came up to Ann as the students were filing out of the room and stopped to ask her a question. "He was really trying to get this clear in his mind. It's great when they keep having questions. That's the biggest compliment, that they'll ask you questions and that they trust you enough to ask you a question. He said, 'So, do you and Linda like to lick each other's pussies?' I said, 'I don't think I need to go into the particular details of my personal sex life, but certainly lesbians, gay men, straight people all enjoy oral sex, and national surveys have shown that it is in fact a favorite form of sexual expression among most people—the majority. Everybody does everything.' He was quite satisfied. He got the information he wanted, which was that everybody does do everything, that it's not just one category of people that does one thing and another category that does another thing. Everybody does everything. That's the message you want to convey."

The National Education Association, the largest teachers' union in the country, supports the effort to teach students about gay and lesbian people and developed a training course to help teachers talk about homosexuality. The organization has also endorsed making gay teen counseling available in every school, a policy that is in part a response to the alarming rate of suicide among gay and lesbian adolescents. Already in a number of cities, high school counseling programs are in place for gay and lesbian teens, including the widely acclaimed—and often attacked—Project 10 in Los Angeles.

The most controversial effort to introduce homosexuality into the school curriculum has taken place in New York City, where a new multicultural curriculum that stresses diversity and tolerance is now in place. The curriculum, called "Children of the Rainbow," addresses the new realities of family life, including gay and lesbian families. But some parents have vigorously objected to the new curriculum because it urges first grade teachers to accentuate the positive aspects of gay relationships as part of general discussions in order to teach students to accept gay and lesbian people. For example, when talking about families in class, the curriculum encourages teachers to include examples of families with two mothers or two fathers.

However strong the objections to teaching students about homosexuality, the reality of AIDS is forcing school boards all across the country to find a way to teach students how to protect themselves from acquiring this deadly disease. The responsible school boards—and one hopes these are in the majority—include in their AIDS education programs blunt discussions of how AIDS can be contracted through both homosexual as well as heterosexual sex, not just vague warnings about avoiding "the exchange of bodily fluids."

■ Do colleges teach courses about homosexuality?

Not long ago, I returned to Vassar for the second Annual Gay and Lesbian Alumnae/i Association Conference. Among the many things that impressed me were the number of professors who participated in the two-day conference, particularly one professor who gave a presentation on a course he was teaching on gays and lesbians in literature. Granted, I've been out of college for a little more than a decade, but the changes are still breathtaking.

When I was a student, there wasn't a single openly gay or lesbian professor. There were teachers I knew were gay, but nobody was open. In fact, I once made the awful mistake of suggesting to a young woman (she was eighteen, and I was twenty) who thought she was a lesbian that she talk to a woman professor I knew was gay, who I thought would do a better job of answering her questions than I could. That was a lesson that needed learning. Though I knew this professor was a lesbian, she wasn't open about it, so I should have asked her if it was okay to have this young woman call her to talk to her about being a lesbian. It was a disaster, because the professor was cold as ice toward this young woman who desperately needed someone to talk to. Now, there are several openly gay or lesbian teachers, advisers, and administrators who would be more than happy to talk to a gay or lesbian undergrad at Vassar.

At the college level, in contrast to high schools, students may first hear about homosexuality during orientation, when all kinds of things are discussed, from where to find a good pizza to safe sex. Courses on gay and lesbian topics, from gay history to gay and lesbian literature, are offered at scores of colleges and universities. Several schools now have gay and lesbian studies departments, including City College of San Francisco, City University of New York, Yale, Harvard, Rutgers, and Duke. And each year hundreds of scholars, students, and activists from around the country gather for the Annual Lesbian, Bisexual, and Gay Studies Conference to debate issues ranging from whether or not there is such a thing as lesbian, bisexual, and gay studies to the origins of homosexuality.

■ What objections do people have to teaching students about homosexuality?

I've heard just about every objection I can think of to teaching students anything about gay and lesbian people, whether it's teaching about gay and lesbian parents or providing straightforward information about AIDS. Usually these objections have been expressed to me by an enraged parent at the top of his or her lungs: "You're trying to recruit our children!" "You want to promote the gay lifestyle!" "How can you teach little children about sick and perverted behavior?" "God created Adam and Eve, not Adam and Steve!" And on and on and on.

But as I explain in chapter 1, "The Basics," and in chapter 11, "Religion," gay and lesbian people do not recruit, do not promote the "gay lifestyle," are not by nature sick and perverted, and many people, including a number of religious leaders, believe that God created gay people just as he created straight people, and loves them just the same.

Every objection confirms for me the importance of teaching children the truth about gay and lesbian people, because it's clear from what I've heard that many parents are going to bestow on a new generation old stereotypes, archaic myths, and ancient fears.

■ Isn't there a gay high school?

The Harvey Milk High School in New York City is a special alternative high school primarily for gay and lesbian youth. It is fully accredited by the New York City Board of Education and is run by the Hetrick-Martin Institute, a nonprofit organization that provides counseling and other services to gay and lesbian youth.

The school, which created quite a stir when it first opened in 1985, was named for Harvey Milk, a gay San Francisco supervisor (city councilman) who was assassinated in 1978.

When you think of a big city high school, you may imagine a great Gothic structure, with school yard, cheerleaders, and thousands of students. This is not the case with Harvey Milk High School, which is located in a couple of rooms at the Hetrick-Martin Institute in lower Manhattan. There are a few dozen students, ages fourteen to twenty-one, mostly boys. There were five graduates in 1992.

The students who attend the Harvey Milk School are kids who had trouble surviving at regular high schools. They were teased about the way they acted or the way they dressed; in some cases they were beaten and abused at the school they came from. The purpose of the Harvey Milk High School is to reintegrate these students into traditional schools or, failing that, to provide them with a safe place where they can come to terms with their lives and get their high school diplomas. It gives them the basics they need to survive in the larger society.

Not everyone has welcomed the idea of a high school for gay and lesbian students, particularly those who still believe that gay people want to "recruit" new members. In reality, the Harvey Milk High School does nothing even close to radical. This was made clear in many interviews by the late Damien Martin, who, along with his lover, the late Emery Hetrick, founded the Hetrick-Martin Institute. He stated that his primary hopes for the students were a sense of self-worth, a diploma, and a job. Regarding the work of the institute itself, he said, "We do exactly what the nuns taught us [in Catholic school]. Feed the hungry, give drink to the thirsty, clothe the naked, shelter the homeless. The corporal and spiritual works of mercy."

▪ Are there openly gay and lesbian schoolteachers?

In places where gay and lesbian people are protected from discrimination in employment—and even in places where they are not—some schoolteachers feel safe enough to be open about who they are. For example, they don't pretend to be straight by bringing opposite-sex escorts to school events and honestly answer their students' questions—for example, "Are you married?" Some cities even have organizations for gay and lesbian teachers.

▪ Do gay and lesbian teachers influence their students to become homosexual?
▪ Are they bad role models?

Gay and lesbian teachers can't influence their students to become homosexual any more than heterosexual teachers can influence their students to become heterosexual. That's because you can't *make* someone gay, lesbian, bisexual, or heterosexual. Openly gay and lesbian teachers can, however, be positive role models to all kids—straight and gay—just as heterosexual teachers can be positive role models to all kids.

Jim teaches in New York City and makes no effort to hide the fact he's gay, nor does he make an effort to hide his frustration with parents who object to his presence in the classroom. "First of all, I don't talk about being gay all the time. What do these parents think I do, walk into class and first thing announce I'm gay and have a lover? It makes me crazy! But if it comes up, I'm not gonna lie about it. And when it's in the news, the kids wanna talk about it. They have questions. Should I tell them to go read a book because I'm not allowed to talk about it, because if I talk about it they'll wanna be gay like me? These parents need to get an education. Look, telling the truth about homosexuals doesn't hurt anyone. I'm educating the straight kids by letting them see a teacher who happens to be gay and does a good job. And the gay and lesbian kids get to see that you can be honest about who you are and have a life and a good career."

Do Jim and other openly gay and lesbian teachers, just by their example, encourage more gay and lesbian young people to come out of the closet? There's every reason to believe that this is the case. But what's the alternative? Should we encourage kids to stay in the closet, hide who they are, and pretend to be straight? If we decide that, then we have to take responsibility for the incredible number of gay and lesbian teenagers who kill themselves because they find their lives impossible to live.

▪ Are there libraries and archives about gay subjects?

A number of libraries around the country, including university libraries, are building substantial gay and lesbian collections. The most ambitious collection is being gathered for the new San Francisco Public Library, which is set to open in 1995 and will house a special gay and lesbian center. From everything I've seen, heard, and read about it, the gay and lesbian center will be an incredible resource.

▪ Are women's colleges all lesbian?

I put this question to a lesbian friend who attended a prestigious all-women's college. Her answer: "Unfortunately, no. I don't even think it's disproportionate." However, some colleges and universities give the impression of having more gay and lesbian students because they offer the kind of supportive community in which gay and lesbian students can feel greater freedom to come out of the closet.

17

POLITICS, ACTIVISM, AND GAY AND LESBIAN RIGHTS

- ### Is homosexuality against the law?

It is not against the law to be a homosexual. However, nearly half the states in the United States have "sodomy laws" that make it illegal for gay and lesbian adults to "perform or submit to any sexual act involving the sex organs of one person and the mouth or anus of another." In some of these states, sodomy laws apply only to people of the same sex. But in the majority of states that have sodomy laws, sexual acts involving the sex organs of one person and the mouth or anus of the other are against the law for both homosexual *and* heterosexual people. These laws are rarely enforced, but when they are, it is almost exclusively in cases involving sex between two men. If these laws were uniformly and aggressively enforced, almost the entire sexually active adult populations of several states would be in jail.

▪ If they are rarely enforced, why are gay and lesbian activists working to overturn sodomy laws?

Although sodomy laws are indeed rarely enforced, gay and lesbian rights leaders argue that these laws encourage discrimination and hate crimes against gay and lesbian people and can be used to restrict career and employment opportunities. For example, before the Texas appeals court ruled in 1992 that the Texas sodomy law was unconstitutional, the Dallas Police Department used it to deny employment to a lesbian applicant. And the fact remains that gay people *have* been arrested, however rarely, for having physical relations in the privacy of their own homes.

Until 1961, all states had laws prohibiting sodomy. Since that time, more than half the states have removed these laws through either legislative action or court decisions. But though plenty of progress has already been made by both straight and gay people to repeal these archaic laws, the Supreme Court in 1987 upheld the right of states to outlaw sexual acts between two people of the same sex.

▪ Why do gay and lesbian people feel they need laws to protect them from discrimination?

The newspaper headlines from recent years say plenty: "Discriminating Against Gay Workers Doesn't Violate a U.S. Law," "Gay Staffer in the Bush Campaign Files Complaint Saying He Was Demoted," "Company Ousts Gay Workers. . ." "FEMA Aide Claims Plot Against Gays," "Writer Ousted After

Saying He's Homosexual," "Recognition Is Refused for Gay Alumni," "Fraternity Rebuff to Homosexual Stirring a Whirlwind in Vermont," "High Court, 5–4, Says States Have the Right to Outlaw Private Homosexual Acts," "Texas Judge Eases Sentence for Killer of 2 Homosexuals," "Judge Rules Scouts Can Block Gay Man as a Troop Leader," "Homosexual, a U.S. Resident 19 Years, Faces Deportation," "Curbs Imposed on Homosexuals as Foster Parents," "Court Rejects Visiting Rights for Former Lesbian Partner."

These headlines offer a few examples of some of the reasons gay and lesbian activists are working for equal rights on the federal, state, and local level. Although life for gay and lesbian people has admittedly improved since the gay rights effort began in the 1950s, it is still perfectly legal in most parts of the country to fire them from their jobs, evict them from their homes, deny them service at restaurants and hotels, and in nearly half the states, arrest them in their own bedrooms for making love with their spouses.

The good news is, gay and lesbian people are currently protected by laws that forbid discrimination in employment, housing, and public accommodation in more than half a dozen states and in scores of municipalities. (The first city to protect the rights of gay people in employment, housing, and public accommodation was Ann Arbor, Michigan, in July 1972.) Major corporations, such as Levi Strauss, AT&T, IBM, Disney, and Citicorp have also adopted policies opposing discrimination against gay and lesbian people in hiring and promotions.

■ What are the arguments against giving gay and lesbian people equal rights?

People who oppose the passage of gay and lesbian equal rights laws at the local, state, and federal level give all kinds of reasons. Some argue that gay men and women are not a class of people—like people classified by race or gender—but simply individuals who engage in sick and sinful behavior, and that such behavior shouldn't be protected by law.

I remember sitting through hearings at New York City Hall for local gay rights legislation in the early 1980s, listening to a city councilman claim that if gay people were given equal rights, the city would be encouraging bestiality and child molestation. Then there were the devoutly religious men in the row behind me who shouted "burn them," every time a gay or lesbian person or supporter came up to the podium to testify. I thought these men, many of whom carried copies of the Bible, made a very compelling case in favor of passing equal rights protection for gay and lesbian people.

Other people argue that gay men and women, like all people, are already guaranteed equal protection under the law by the Constitution and therefore don't need any "special rights." But the fact is, in most places in the nation, gay and lesbian people do not have equal protection under the law. For example, let's say the company I work for decides to fire me because I'm gay. They've been happy with my work, and in fact, just gave me a raise. But they found out from one of my colleagues that I'm gay and don't want gay people working for them. At the same time they fire me, they decide to fire one of my colleagues because they've decided that they don't want black people working for the company any longer. In most places in the United States I would have no recourse, because in most places, it is perfectly legal to fire someone simply because they're gay or lesbian. I could not sue my employer to regain my job. My colleague, on the other hand, could sue because federal civil rights laws forbid discrimination based on race, among other things.

All that gay and lesbian people are asking for are the same legal protections most Americans take for granted, including protection from discrimination in employment, housing, and public accommodation. These are not "special rights," and the people who promote this antigay "special rights" argument know that gay and lesbian people are working for "equal rights." But the "special rights" argument has proven effective in defeating and repealing gay rights legislation, because no one wants any group of people to have "special rights."

One of my favorite arguments from people who say that gay and lesbian people are asking for "special rights" is that gay men in particular are already so successful—apparently we all drive expensive cars and live in sprawling, well-appointed homes—that we couldn't possibly need any extra protection.

■ Do gay people discriminate?

Gay and lesbian people discriminate in all the ways that heterosexual people do, based on race, gender, physical appearance, age—you name it. Deborah Johnson, who is a consultant to many gay and lesbian rights organizations, remembers the racial discrimination she experienced during the mid-1980s. "The most blatant kinds I encountered during those years were the exclusionary policies at the gay clubs. If you were black, you could only get in on a certain night. We used to call it 'Plantation Night.' We used to picket all the time. On the nights when blacks weren't welcome, which was most nights, they made blacks show two or three picture IDs. How many people carry three picture IDs?"

I like the observation made by Martin Block, an early gay activist, about bias among the gay men in his organization, the Mattachine Society, in the early 1950s. "Anytime there was a proposal to do something public, people argued, 'Well, I don't want those drag queens coming' or 'I don't want that one coming' or 'Isn't she outrageous with her constant swish?' I'm not saying that drag queens were not welcome. I'm saying that they were not welcome by everybody. In every gay movement there has always been a schism. Some people don't want anyone who sticks his little pinky out, and some people don't want anyone who doesn't stick his little pinky out. None of us is without bias. And I am delighted to say that I am full of bias myself, but my bias is mostly against stupidity."

■ When did the gay civil rights movement start?

Today's national, high-profile, and very vocal gay and lesbian equal rights movement began in California in the 1950s with the formation of a number of organizations, including the Mattachine Society, founded in Los Angeles in 1950, and the Daughters of Bilitis, an organization for lesbians founded in San Francisco in 1955. These fledgling groups had very modest goals that were a reflection of their tiny memberships, their modest resources, the intensely antigay climate of the times, and the overwhelming fear almost all gay and lesbian people had of being found out.

Other than providing discussion groups where gay and lesbian people could meet one another and talk about the problems they faced, these organizations fought for the right of gay and lesbian people to assemble in bars without being harassed or arrested by the police, and they published the first widely circulated magazines for gay and lesbian people.

■ Wasn't the Stonewall riot in New York City in 1969 the beginning of the gay rights movement?

When I first began work on *Making History*, my book about the history of the gay and lesbian rights struggle, I thought, like most other gay people, that the gay rights movement began in June 1969 with a riot that followed a routine police raid at the Stonewall Inn, a gay bar in New York City's Greenwich Village.

Soon after I started my research, I discovered that by the time of the Stonewall riot, there was already a national, active movement of more than forty gay and lesbian organizations. Though the Stonewall riot was not the beginning, it was, without question, a major turning point in the struggle. It dramatically energized the gay and lesbian rights movement and inspired the formation of scores of new gay and lesbian rights groups across the country.

■ Why do gay people speak about gay pride?

Being proud of one's sexual orientation may seem strange to heterosexual people, for whom sexual orientation is a relative nonissue. But as educator Ann Northrop explained, "Homosexuals are taught from preconsciousness to be ashamed of themselves and to hate themselves and to think that they are disgusting, aberrant, immoral human beings. So the achievement of any kind of self-esteem in a lesbian or gay person is an incredible victory against almost insurmountable odds in the society we live in. Those of us who have achieved any small measure of self-esteem celebrate and take pride in the extent to which we've been able to achieve it. When you've been given the exact opposite all your life, there is a great need to achieve a sense of pride."

Ann pointed out that heterosexual people, too, express pride in their heterosexuality, whether or not they realize it, by having weddings, wearing wedding rings, or placing marriage announcements in newspapers. "What is a wedding except a prideful celebration of heterosexuality?" she added.

■ Why do gay people have marches every year in June?

The annual gay and lesbian marches, which are held in cities across the United States and in other countries around the world during the month of June, commemorate the June 28, 1969, Stonewall riot. Beyond this shared anniversary, each local parade committee sets its own theme, which may range from gay and lesbian freedom to gay and lesbian pride. In addition, each of the thousands of participating groups have their own reasons for marching. And the hundreds of thousands of people who participate in the parades have their own reasons for marching as well. Some people march as a show of political strength, to celebrate gay and lesbian pride, to demand equal rights, or all of the above. Others march in support of their gay and lesbian children or parents, or to celebrate freedom from the confines of the closet. Others still are just there to have a good time in their favorite costumes. One young woman, who has been marching in New York City's gay and lesbian parade for the past three years, gave this reason for marching: "It's the one day a year I can walk down the street in broad daylight with my arm around my lover's shoulder and get cheered for it instead of having people spit at us."

Today's gay and lesbian marches are a direct descendent of an annual protest march first held on July 4, 1965, in front of Independence Hall in Philadelphia. The annual picket was staged by a couple of dozen very courageous lesbians and gay men who carried signs demanding equal rights for homosexuals.

Martha Shelley, a major gay rights leader in the late 1960s and early 1970s, participated in the Independence Hall protest two years in a row. "I thought it was something that might possibly have an effect," she recalled. "I remember walking around in my little white blouse and skirt and tourists standing there eating their ice-cream cones and watching us like the zoo had opened."

Though most Americans have now seen gay and lesbian people on television, in newspaper and magazine photographs, and in person, when the Independence Hall protests were started, most people had never seen someone who they knew was a living, breathing homosexual.

The Independence Hall annual picket continued through 1969, the year of the Stonewall riot. The following year, the

July 4 Independence Hall picket was discontinued. Instead, a few thousand protesters marched in New York City on June 28 to commemorate the Stonewall riot, celebrate gay pride, and demand equal rights. Over a thousand protesters also marched that same day in Los Angeles.

▪ Does the gay rights movement have its own Rosa Parks?

Though there is only one Rosa Parks, Dr. Evelyn Hooker, a pioneering research psychologist, has been called by some people "the Rosa Parks of the gay rights movement."

Dr. Hooker, who is heterosexual, conducted a courageous study in the 1950s in which she compared the psychological profiles of thirty homosexual men and thirty heterosexual men. Dr. Hooker concluded that, contrary to the widely held belief that homosexuality was a mental illness, there were no significant differences between the two groups. Her findings ultimately led to the removal of homosexuality from the American Psychiatric Association's list of mental illnesses in 1973. This change in classification was one of the most important steps in the struggle for gay and lesbian equal rights.

▪ What kinds of political organizations do gay men and lesbians have?

There are all kinds of organizations dedicated to working for gay and lesbian equal rights, from college student groups and political action committees to legal organizations and political clubs.

▪ What is ACT UP?

The AIDS Coalition to Unleash Power, or ACT UP, is a direct-action organization dedicated to confronting the issues of discrimination against people with HIV infection and access to experimental AIDS drugs. It was founded in 1987 in New York City by author and playwright Larry Kramer to force the government, businesses, and the public to confront the AIDS crisis. This civil disobedience organization, with more than a hundred chapters in the United States and abroad, has succeeded in pressuring the Food and Drug Administration to speed up the process of testing and releasing potentially useful AIDS drugs, convinced drug companies to lower prices of AIDS drugs, and focused public and media attention on the worldwide health crisis.

Most of the people involved in ACT UP are gay or lesbian and relatively young. Many ACT UP members have AIDS themselves, have tested positive for HIV, or have lost a loved one to the disease.

▪ What is Queer Nation?

Queer Nation was organized in New York City in 1990 by several members of ACT UP who wanted to focus their energy specifically on gay and lesbian rights issues. "We wanted to do direct action, to get out on the streets, to scream and yell, to stage very visible protests against antigay violence and discrimination," said one of the group's founders. Queer Nation has many chapters across the country.

▪ Why do some gay and lesbian people wear a pink triangle?

A pink inverted triangle symbol (point down) was first used by the Nazis during World War II to identify homosexuals in concentration camps. (Jews had to wear a yellow Star of David.) During the 1970s, as more became known about the persecution and murder of thousands of homosexuals by the Nazis, gay and lesbian people began wearing the inverted pink triangle symbol to publicly identify themselves as homosexuals, as a symbol of pride, and as a way of commemorating those who died in the concentration camps.

▪ What does the rainbow flag stand for?

The six-stripe flag, representing the colors of the rainbow, is a symbol of gay and lesbian pride. According to the *Alyson Almanac*, the rainbow flag was designed and made in 1978 by San Franciscan Gilbert Baker. The rainbow flag is displayed throughout the year in neighborhoods where large numbers of gay and lesbian people live and in gay- and lesbian-owned stores, and it's also displayed at gay and lesbian marches and celebrations throughout the world.

▪ Are all gay and lesbian people liberals?

Because the vast majority of visible and politically active gay and lesbian people are relatively liberal, there is the mistaken impression that all gay and lesbian people are Democrats and support liberal causes. But, in fact, there are plenty of gay and lesbian people who identify themselves as Republicans and more than just a few gay men and women who are very conservative, including Marvin Liebman, a founder of the modern conservative movement.

▪ Did the FBI keep files on homosexuals?

Throughout the 1950s, 1960s, and early 1970s, gay and lesbian rights leaders claimed that the FBI was keeping a close eye on their activities. Some people thought this was simply paranoia. It wasn't. According to Randy Shilts, a journalist who thoroughly researched internal FBI memorandums, "The FBI conducted exhaustive and apparently illegal surveillance of the gay rights movement and its leaders for more than two decades. The surveillance started in 1953 and was continuing as late as 1975. Agents made extensive use of informants, tape-recorded meetings, collected lists of members of gay organizations, photographed participants in early homosexual rights marches, and investigated advertisers in gay publications."

18

AIDS

▪ What is AIDS?

AIDS (acquired immunodeficiency syndrome) is a disease of the immune system that eventually destroys the body's ability to fight other diseases. AIDS is caused by a virus, HIV (human immunodeficiency virus), which can be transmitted when blood, semen, or vaginal secretions containing the virus are passed from one body to another through, for example, unprotected vaginal or anal intercourse, or through intravenous drug use when needles are shared.

I remember being very alarmed by the first article I read in the *New York Times* about forty-one gay men who had been diagnosed with a rare form of cancer. That was the summer of 1981, and those perplexing cancer cases were just the very beginning of what became the AIDS epidemic. By the early 1990s, in the United States alone, AIDS had claimed the lives of well over one hundred thousand people, more than half of them gay men. The World Health Organization now calculates that HIV will infect up to 40 million people—men and women, adults and children, straight and gay—worldwide by the year 2000.

▪ Did gay men cause AIDS?

AIDS is caused by HIV, a virus, not someone's sexual orientation, and it is spread in a number of ways, not just by one kind of sexual act.

▪ Is AIDS a gay disease?

AIDS is a human disease, and in most parts of the world it's a predominantly heterosexual disease. In the United States, where AIDS first spread among gay men in major urban areas, the majority of those already infected with HIV (as of the early 1990s) were gay men. But with each passing day, gay men make up a smaller and smaller percentage of total AIDS cases in the United States as the disease continues to spread.

▪ Do lesbians get AIDS?

Lesbians get AIDS just like everybody else, although female-to-female transmission of HIV through sex is rare.

▪ How do lesbians get AIDS through sex with other women?

AIDS is caused by HIV, a virus, which is in the blood, semen, and vaginal fluids of an infected person. HIV can penetrate mucous membranes that line the vagina, mouth, and other parts of the body. So if one woman has the virus, she carries it in her vaginal fluids. If her sexual partner gets some of these vaginal fluids in her vagina or mouth, it's possible for her to become infected with HIV.

▪ If one partner in a male couple has AIDS, won't the other partner get it?

You can't get AIDS through casual everyday contact with someone who has the disease. So unless the two men do something that can spread the virus, that is, have unsafe sex (for example, anal intercourse without proper use of a condom) or share needles, the healthy partner will remain free of HIV.

▪ What impact has AIDS had on gay people?

The most immediate and tragic impact of AIDS on gay people has been the death of tens of thousands of gay men. But the epidemic has had other effects as well, from increased discrimination against gay people and unprecedented media attention, to the mobilization of more gay men and lesbians on a single issue than at any time in the history of the struggle for gay and lesbian equal rights. Many of these men and women had never before been involved in any organization that had anything to do with gay people.

One of the people drawn into activism by the AIDS crisis was Sara Boesser from Juneau, Alaska, who is now a leading gay rights activist in her state. Sara had always planned one day to become a gay rights activist, but not until she was an "old fart." Long before she became an old fart, Sara started reading stories about people with AIDS. "There were horror stories about how AIDS patients were not only dying, but were also being abandoned by their families, losing their jobs, and losing their insurance. There was even fear that there would be legislation to quarantine homosexuals. Some people considered AIDS to be an issue for the men only, but from what I read, it seemed that homosexual rights in general were at stake. It occurred to me that if the men lost their rights, I'd lose mine. So with the coming of AIDS, I realized I couldn't postpone forever what was important to me, because I might not get to be an old fart. I had to take my stand today because tomorrow might not be here."

Besides bringing people together to fight AIDS and fight for gay rights, the AIDS epidemic has also led to a significant new rift, between those infected with HIV and those who are not. For example, those who are infected with HIV often have different priorities when it comes to battling AIDS and lobbying for gay rights than people who are not infected.

■ How has AIDS resulted in more discrimination against gay people?

Because many people have mistakenly blamed gay men for the AIDS epidemic and labeled them as disease carriers, AIDS has given many people an excuse to openly discriminate against and physically attack gay people. For example, people with AIDS and those suspected of being infected with HIV have had their insurance revoked, been fired from their jobs, and been evicted from their homes. In addition, same-sex partners have been denied access to their ill lovers and excluded from funerals by the families of their deceased lovers.

One of the major examples of increased discrimination specifically against gay men is that of insurance companies that have tried to screen out all gay men in an attempt to avoid underwriting policies for those presumed to be at risk for AIDS. One company, which was forced through a lawsuit to stop screening for sexual orientation, required its agents to distribute a questionnaire to all unmarried male applicants with "occupations that do not require physical exertion," such as "restaurant employees, antique dealers, interior decorators, consultants, florists, and people in the jewelry and fashion business." The questionnaire, designed to identify which of these men were gay, included general queries about health as well as specific questions concerning treatment for sexually transmitted diseases or immune disorders. A "yes" response to any of the questions resulted in a denial of insurance coverage.

■ Has AIDS set back the struggle for gay and lesbian equal rights?

At the very beginning of the AIDS crisis, many gay and lesbian rights activists feared that negative publicity about AIDS would lead to the loss of hard-won rights. But despite their worst fears and the tragic number of deaths from AIDS, including the deaths of many leaders within the gay and lesbian rights movement, AIDS has helped move the gay rights effort in a positive direction in a number of ways.

People with AIDS were fired from jobs, evicted from their homes, and denied health insurance, helping throw into sharp focus many of the discrimination issues that gay and lesbian rights leaders have been screaming about for years and very clearly demonstrating the need for laws protecting gay people from discrimination. In addition, after they had been almost entirely ignored by the mainstream press, AIDS dramatically increased the visibility of gay and lesbian people by putting them in the news almost daily. And thousands of gay men and lesbians who had never participated in gay rights efforts were motivated to join the fight against AIDS. Many of these people, who now have extensive experience organizing, fund-raising, and working with elected officials, have gone on to work on gay and lesbian rights issues.

■ What is ACT UP?

See chapter 17, "Politics, Activism, and Gay and Lesbian Rights."

▪ How has AIDS changed the public's awareness of gay people?

For years, gay and lesbian rights activists have said that if all the gay and lesbian people in the country turned lavender for one day that would be the end of discrimination against gay people, because all Americans would realize that they knew and loved someone who was gay or lesbian. Though that might not mean the complete end of discrimination, it certainly would shake up a few people and force them to reevaluate their beliefs.

AIDS didn't turn all gay men and lesbians lavender, but AIDS has revealed to millions of people—family, friends, colleagues, neighbors—that they know and love, or have known and loved, someone who is gay. It's also been revealed, through their tragic deaths, that many beloved celebrities were gay.

The AIDS crisis has also focused unprecedented media attention on gay and lesbian people. This attention has given those not immediately affected by the AIDS crisis an opportunity to see that gay men have loving companions, friends, and often supportive families, and that gay and lesbian people are compassionate, hardworking, and courageous people, as they've organized to spread information about preventing AIDS, taken care of the sick and dying, and lobbied for increased spending for AIDS research and swift approval of experimental drugs.

▪ Who are some famous people who were gay and have died from AIDS?

Actors Rock Hudson, Anthony Perkins, and Robert Reed (Mike Brady from "The Brady Bunch"); entertainers Liberace and Peter Allen; attorney Roy Cohn, Washington Redskins tight end Jerry Smith, designer Willi Smith, photographer Robert Mapplethorpe, dancer Rudolf Nureyev, artist Keith

Haring, congressman Stewart McKinney—the list goes on and on and on.

▪ Why are gay men still getting AIDS?

Because AIDS has such a long incubation period (the time between infection and onset of symptoms) many of the gay men being diagnosed with AIDS today were infected with HIV long before anyone knew what caused the disease and how to prevent it.

There are also, of course, gay men who were infected with HIV and diagnosed with AIDS well after we knew how to prevent HIV infection. Some of these men have had unsafe sex or shared needles during IV drug use. Others have followed safe sex recommendations, but because condoms are not foolproof and can break, they've contracted the virus despite their efforts not to.

▪ Why do gay men have unsafe sex?

I had a conversation not long ago with an acquaintance who is very well educated, in the heart of middle age, and a real enthusiast about life. He told me a story about how he had unprotected anal intercourse with a young man he had just met. My jaw was already on the floor before he got to the part where he told me, "And he ejaculated inside me." I was astonished— no, horrified. "How," I asked, "could you do that?" This man, who has read all the same articles I have and knows people who have died from AIDS said, "It felt like the right thing to do. I trusted him. He told me that he'd tested negative." Right, and the check is in the mail.

In the heat of passion, people—gay and straight, young and old—are not always entirely rational, especially when alcohol and/or drugs are part of the mixture. So sometimes even people who know better don't have safe sex. This is especially true of young people, who tend to feel immortal. But besides thinking they'll live forever, many young gay men view AIDS as a disease that belongs to an older generation of gay men. Also, because younger men most often don't know anyone who has AIDS or has died from AIDS, and think they don't know anyone infected with HIV, they believe that they're free from risk of infection.

Other gay men don't practice safe sex because they can't acknowledge to themselves that they're gay and engaging in sex with other men, even if that's what they're doing. Because they don't think they're gay, and AIDS is a "gay disease," they can't possibly be at risk. This kind of thinking may sound farfetched, but there are many men in very deep denial about who they are and what they're doing. This is an especially acute problem for black and Hispanic men, who are even more reluctant than white men to acknowledge that they're gay because of the even more extreme condemnation of homosexuality in their communities.

Whatever the specific reason for having unsafe sex, gay men—and lesbians, and straight people—are only human, and humans do all kinds of things they know are dangerous, like smoking, driving without a seat belt, and drinking too much. Everyone likes to believe, "It won't happen to me."

▪ Where can I get more information on AIDS and safe sex?

Everyone needs to know about AIDS and how to prevent infection with HIV. You can talk to your doctor, call a local health organization, or call a local or national AIDS hotline. The telephone number for the National AIDS Hotline, which is staffed twenty-four hours a day, is 1-800-342-AIDS.

19

AGING

▪ Are there old gay and lesbian people?

When I first found my way into the gay world in New York City in the mid-1970s, my impression was that "old" gay people were around twenty-five or thirty years old. I rarely saw anyone much older, and certainly I never saw anyone over the age of fifty.

Where were all the older gay and lesbian people? For the most part, they were invisible. Gay and lesbian people now in their seventies, eighties, and older grew up in a world that almost uniformly condemned them, a world in which no one spoke of coming out of the closet, because being open about your homosexuality was both unimaginable and dangerous. It's not surprising, then, having spent a life in hiding, that very few of the millions of older gay and lesbian people have come forward.

▪ Are there old gay and lesbian couples?

Most are well hidden, but there are gay and lesbian couples across the country who have been living together for thirty, forty, fifty, or more years. Given how hostile the world used to be toward gay and lesbian people, it's remarkable that any such couple relationships managed to survive into old age.

▪ Is it harder growing old if you're gay or lesbian?

Most older gay and lesbian people, men and women in their sixties, seventies, and eighties are frightened of being found out and are even more isolated than their heterosexual counterparts. Most spent their lives hiding their sexual identity and their relationships, and most plan to take their secret to the grave despite today's more liberal attitudes.

Two older gay and lesbian people I've gotten to know well, Paul and Linda, have shared their secret with only a handful of gay friends, most of whom are now dead. Paul, who is nearly ninety, would like to let the people in his church know that he's gay, but he's afraid they'll think less of him if they know the truth. "I've known I was homosexual since my teens, but I've always felt bad about it," said Paul, who lives by himself in an apartment complex for senior citizens in Denver. "I'd like to say something, but what if they don't accept me? What will I do then?"

Paul told me that he would like to find a companion, "not for a physical relationship—I can't do that anymore. But for the company." He asked me, "Do you think it's too late for me to meet someone?"

Linda, who is nearly eighty, lives in a small bungalow just outside Seattle with her two dogs and four cats. Only the two "gay boys" who live across the street from her know that she's a lesbian. "I think they knew I was gay soon after they moved in. I still haven't asked them how they could tell. We've gotten friendly over the past few years, and now we always share articles and books that talk about gays. Last week they drove me to the vet. One of the dogs was sick. I'm lucky to have them. It's funny, they tell me they're lucky to have *me.*"

For some gay and lesbian people, the sense of isolation can be extreme. They may have shared their secret with only one person, a long-term lover. After the death of that lover, these men and women have no one with whom to share their lives and reminiscences and no one with whom they can be completely honest.

Old age, for many gay and lesbian people, also means having to deal with social service agencies and health care providers that may have no experience dealing with gay and lesbian people. This can be especially difficult for couples, who may be very reluctant to reveal the special relationship they have with their "best friend" or "housemate." Imagine, for example, the challenge faced by a woman who needs to find a nursing home for her long-term lover who is suffering from severe memory loss. Because she and her lover are just close friends—as far as the nursing home knows—they will be treated differently from a heterosexual married couple. And unless she and her lover have completed the necessary legal documents, the healthy partner will not be able to make medical and financial decisions for her ill longtime companion.

■ Are there retirement homes specifically for gay people?

No, but a number of people I've talked to over the past few years have investigated the feasibility of starting retirement homes for gay and lesbian elderly people and are trying to raise funds for such a project. The purpose of these retirement homes, as one fund-raising brochure states, is to provide a residential facility for older gay men and lesbians "whose needs in their later years are not being met by the existing, often non-sympathetic, nonunderstanding administrators and personnel." The brochure goes on to explain that although many of the needs of gay and lesbian elderly people are similar to those of other senior citizens, gay and lesbian senior citizens "often lack family and offspring supports."

Though retirement homes specifically for gay and lesbian senior citizens don't yet exist, many care providers are beginning to address the fact that not all senior citizens are heterosexual. One social worker I spoke with, who works with nursing homes to make them aware of the special needs of gay and lesbian residents, told me that most nursing homes have a very long way to go before they deal realistically with the issue of homosexuality. She described one experience that she said was all too typical. "It was a Jewish home in New York City. I spoke with one of the directors and explained that I wanted to come in and talk about the special needs of his gay and lesbian clients. He quickly responded, 'We're a Jewish home.' Does he think that there aren't any gay Jews? That's the biggest problem I face, convincing people that, number one, there are gay and lesbian senior citizens out there, and, number two, that we have to learn how to reach out to them."

▪ Are there organizations for old gay and lesbian people?

There are organizations for gay and lesbian senior citizens in most major cities. The oldest and best known organization, SAGE—Senior Action in a Gay Environment—is located in New York City. It provides a range of services to elderly gay men and lesbians, including home, hospital, and institutional visiting, transportation to doctors, weekly workshops and discussion groups, and monthly parties.

▪ What do grandchildren think of their gay grandparents?

Some people have trouble adjusting to the idea that Grandma is a lesbian or Grandpa is gay. And others love their grandparents just the same.

In an interview in the *New York Times* several years ago, a seventy-nine-year-old woman, who asked to be identified as Gerry, said that when she told her daughter about her secret life, her daughter told her grandchildren, "Grandma's gay." According to the interview, "Gerry said that the kids looked at their mother and remarked, 'So what else is new?' Gerry smiled and said, 'It made me feel like I was only seventy years old.' "

▪ Do gay people take care of elderly parents?

There are no statistics on the number of gay and lesbian people who are taking care of elderly parents, but plenty do it.

Craig and Mitchell, lovers for two decades, have looked after Craig's mother since she moved in with them five years ago. He joked, "I think God created gay and lesbian people because someone had to take care of the elderly parents. My sister and brother can't do it because they have kids. So it's up to me, the gay son." Craig's mother has known about the nature of her son's relationship with Mitchell for almost as long as they've been together. Mitchell said that she treats him just like her own son, "which isn't always a good thing."

20

MORE QUESTIONS . . .

- **What is a transvestite?**
- **Are all transvestites gay men?**
- **What is a drag queen?**

A transvestite is technically someone who dresses in the clothing of the opposite gender and for whom that dressing is sexually exciting. Most transvestites are heterosexual men, and they do their cross-dressing in secret or only in the company of other heterosexual transvestites.

People who dress up in clothing of the opposite gender for a costume party, a play, or just for fun are "cross-dressing" or dressing in "drag." A gay man who does this is sometimes called a "drag queen." A man who dresses as a woman to perform professionally in public is called a female impersonator.

▪ What is a drag ball?

Many people got a close look at one type of drag ball in Jennie Livingston's remarkable award-winning documentary film, *Paris Is Burning*. In it, Livingston introduced viewers to Harlem drag balls, where black and Hispanic gay men and women dress up to compete for trophies in different categories. In the "Realness" category, for example, gay men try to "pass" as straight schoolboys, executives, street thugs, soldiers, and beautiful, glamorous women.

Another type of drag ball is held in the context of the Imperial Court System, which is one of the oldest and largest gay charitable organizations. Dating back to the early 1960s, the several dozen individual "courts" of the Imperial Court System around the country hold fund-raising balls to benefit both local and national gay, as well as straight, charities. People who attend these balls, primarily gay men, dress in all kinds of formal attire. For example, the instruction booklet for the high camp "Night of a Thousand Gowns" charity ball held at the Waldorf-Astoria Hotel by the Imperial Court of New York states, "Full court dress is preferred: elegant gowns with tiaras, orders, and family jewels, and/or white tie and tails (knee breeches with silver buckles, for those with the legs for it). Black tie is acceptable, though there is always the possibility of your being mistaken for a waiter. Military personnel may wear dress uniform with full regimentals; swords are optional (but dueling is prohibited)."

▪ Who are the Sisters of Perpetual Indulgence?

The Sisters of Perpetual Indulgence, a group of San Francisco gay men who dress as nuns, first appeared on the scene in 1979. They chose nun drag, according to a profile of the Sisters in the *San Francisco Chronicle*, because "they saw the Catholic church as a 'bulwark of oppression.'"

The Sisters, who can be spotted at the annual gay pride march in San Francisco, have been involved in everything from producing one of the earliest safe sex brochures and distributing tens of thousands of condoms in the fight against AIDS to fund-raising for various gay and lesbian causes.

One of the most famous sisters, Sister Boom Boom, the creation of San Franciscan Jack Fertig, actually ran for city government, winning twenty-three thousand votes in a 1982 city supervisor's race. She was easily identified by her nun's habit, oversized foam rubber breasts, false eyelashes, and stiletto heels.

▪ Why do some gay people dress up in black leather?

Sometimes gay and lesbian people, just like heterosexual people, wear black leather garments—pants, jacket, boots, and so on—simply because they like to wear black leather. It may be nothing more than a fashion statement. (Black leather is currently the costume of choice for many fashion-conscious young people, regardless of sexual orientation.) For other gay and lesbian people, black leather garments and accessories are an indication that they engage in S & M (sadism and masochism) role playing and/or sex. Their black leather garments are part of a uniform that is recognized by other people who are a part of the "leather community." (However, not all people who engage in S & M dress in black leather.)

▪ How do other countries deal with gay and lesbian people?

When I traveled through Europe as a student, I made a trip to what was then the Soviet Union. Prior to leaving for Europe, I had a look through a gay guide to Europe just to get a sense of where I could hope to find other gay people. I'll never forget turning to the chapter on the Soviet Union. It was just one page and had one sentence. The situation for gay people in the Soviet Union was apparently so dangerous that the authors of the guide wrote something like, "Don't even *think* about it while you're in the Soviet Union."

Obviously, a lot has changed since 1979. The Soviet Union is no more. Russia, the largest of the former Soviet republics, now has a nascent gay rights movement, and Russian president Boris Yeltsin has proposed lifting the ban on sexual relations between two men. (There is no law in Russia against two women having sex.) The situation in some of the former Soviet republics is brighter. In Latvia and Ukraine, for example, homosexual relations have already been decriminalized.

Around the world, the situation for gay and lesbian people varies by country and region. In general, European countries have very liberal attitudes toward homosexuality. Denmark, for example, allows gay and lesbian couples to legally marry. But in other parts of the world, particularly Asia and Africa, gay and lesbian people face enormous oppression and even fear for their lives. In Iran, for example, homosexual acts are illegal for both men and women and are punishable by death.

Many countries have no laws that forbid or permit homosexual relations, but that doesn't mean gay and lesbian people can lead their lives in a climate free from prejudice or harm. In China, homosexuals are treated for what most doctors there consider a mental illness. Two of the most popular methods used in China to "cure" homosexuality, according to a story published in the *New York Times,* are the application of painful electric shocks or induced vomiting to discourage erotic thoughts. On the bright side, the article goes on to note that though most Chinese frown on homosexuality, it is considered in poor taste or improper rather than sinful. There are also "no common insults in Chinese related to sexual orientation."

▪ Are there as many gay people in other countries as there are in the United States?

The same percentage of people the world over have feelings of sexual attraction for those of the same sex. The primary differences are how people choose to express—or not express—these feelings, and how different governments choose to deal with their gay and lesbian citizens.

▪ Can gay and lesbian foreigners become U.S. citizens?

Until 1990, federal law barred people "with psychopathic personality, or sexual deviation, or a mental defect" from even entering the United States. This law was used to bar entry of homosexual aliens, and it was upheld in 1967, when the U.S. Supreme Court ruled that homosexuals could be barred from the country as sexual deviants.

In November 1990, President Bush signed into law an immigration reform bill that included the elimination of restrictions based on sexual orientation. Unfortunately, that law did not include easing the restriction on those infected with HIV who wish to enter the country.

▪ Why do some gay people have piercings and tattoos?

In recent years, piercings—pierced ears, noses, nipples, lips, and so on—and tattoos have grown more popular, particularly among some groups of both straight and gay young people. People who choose to pierce their body parts or adorn their bodies with tattoos do so for various reasons.

One young man I talked to, who has several tattoos, said that by marking his body, "I can express my individuality in a way I can't with clothes or a haircut." A woman I spoke with agreed, adding that her tattoos and piercings showed her "tribal allegiance." "Between my clothes, haircut, tattoos, and piercings, I get my point across that I'm a member of the tribe."

▪ Are gay men more sensitive than straight men?

Some gay men are sensitive. And so are some straight men. But are gay men inherently more sensitive than straight men? One theory I've heard over the years is that gay men are in general more sensitive than straight men because the experience of growing up gay—being an outsider—gives many gay men more insight about life, making them more sensitive than the average heterosexual to the challenges faced by other people. It's a nice theory, and I even think it has some merit, but what about all the gay men who are just as insensitive as the most insensitive heterosexual men?

▪ Why are so many gay men fans of opera?

I've tried. I've really tried, but I can't get through *La Bohème;* I always fall asleep during the third act. And with Janáček's *Katia Kabanova,* I couldn't make it through the first act, and that despite the fact I flew to Chicago to hear a friend who was singing a leading role. Fortunately she didn't glance down into the front row—she had gotten us house seats—and see me with my head slumped over.

There are many gay men who are major opera fans (also known within the community as "opera queens"), but there are also many straight men and women as well as lesbians who are opera fans.

▪ Why do some women performers attract a large gay male following?

After posing this question to several people, both straight and gay, I found that the only thing all of them could agree on was that people like Judy Garland, Joan Crawford, Barbra Streisand, Bette Midler, Bette Davis, Marilyn Monroe, and Liza Minnelli were popular with an apparently large number of gay men. Several offered the explanation that the gay men who are fans of these women are attracted to the combined strength and vulnerability these women project(ed) in their work.

Other people offered all kinds of explanations, none of which held up to even gentle follow-up questioning. Any suggestions?

▪ Do gay people have an impact on popular culture?

Gay and lesbian people have long had a major influence on popular culture, from the clothes people wear and the advertisements we see to the kind of music people dance to and the stories we read.

I like what the writer Fran Lebowitz has said on this subject: "If you removed all the homosexuals and homosexual influence from what is generally regarded as American culture, you would be pretty much left with 'Let's Make a Deal.' "

BIBLIOGRAPHY

The Alyson Almanac: A Treasury of Information for the Gay and Lesbian Community. Boston: Alyson Publications, 1990.

Barrett, Martha Barron. *Invisible Lives: The Truth About Millions of Women-Loving Women*. New York: Harper Perennial, 1990.

Berube, Allan. *Coming Out Under Fire: The History of Gay Men and Women in World War Two*. New York: The Free Press, 1990.

Berzon, Betty. *Permanent Partners: Building Gay and Lesbian Relationships That Last*. New York: Plume, 1990.

———, ed. *Positively Gay: New Approaches to Gay and Lesbian Life*. Berkeley, CA: Celestial Arts, 1992.

Blumenthal, Warren J. *Homophobia: How We All Pay the Price*. Boston: Beacon Press, 1992.

Borhek, Mary V. *My Son Eric: A Mother Struggles to Accept Her Gay Son and Discovers Herself*. New York: Pilgrim Press, 1979.

———. *Coming Out to Parents: A Two-Way Survival Guide for Lesbians and Gay Men and Their Parents*. New York: Pilgrim Press, 1983.

Boswell, John. *Christianity, Social Tolerance, and Homosexuality: Gay People in Western Europe from the Beginning of the Christian Era to the Fourteenth Century*. Chicago: Univ. of Chicago Press, 1980.

Bright, Susie. *Susie Sexpert's Lesbian Sex World*. Pittsburgh: Cleis Press, 1990.

Buxton, Amity Pierce. *The Other Side of the Closet: The Coming-Out Crisis for Straight Spouses.* Santa Monica, CA: IBS Press, 1991.

Curry, Hayden, and Clifford, Denis. *A Legal Guide for Lesbian and Gay Couples.* Berkeley, CA: Nolo Press, 1991.

D'Emilio, John. *Sexual Politics, Sexual Communities: The Making of a Homosexual Minority in the United States, 1940–1970.* Chicago: Univ. of Chicago Press, 1983.

Duberman, Martin; Vicinus, Martha; and Chauncey, George, Jr. *Hidden from History: Reclaiming the Gay and Lesbian Past.* New York: NAL Books, 1989.

Eichberg, Rob. *Coming Out: An Act of Love.* New York: Plume, 1991.

Faderman, Lillian. *Odd Girls and Twilight Lovers: A History of Lesbian Life in Twentieth-Century America.* New York: Columbia Univ. Press, 1991.

Fairchild, Betty, and Hayward, Nancy. *Now That You Know.* New York: Harcourt Brace Jovanovich, 1979.

Fricke, Aaron. *Reflections of a Rock Lobster: A Story About Growing Up Gay.* Boston: Alyson Publications, 1981.

Griffin, Carolyn Welch; Wirth, Marian J.; and Wirth, Arthur G. *Beyond Acceptance: Parents of Lesbians and Gays Talk About Their Experiences.* Englewood Cliffs, NJ: Prentice-Hall, 1986.

Heger, Heinz. *The Men with the Pink Triangle.* Boston: Alyson Publications, 1980.

Herek, Gregory M. *Hate Crimes: Confronting Violence Against Lesbians and Gay Men.* Newbury Park, CA: Sage Publications, 1992.

Heron, Ann. *One Teenager in Ten: Writings by Gay and Lesbian Youth.* Boston: Alyson Publications, 1983.

Hobson, Laura Z. *Consenting Adult.* New York: Warner Books, 1976.

Hunter, Nan D.; Michaelson, Sherryl E.; and Stoddard, Thomas B. *The Rights of Lesbians and Gay Men: The Basic ACLU Guide to Gay Person's Rights.* 3d ed. Carbondale: Southern Illinois Univ. Press, 1992.

Hutchings, Loraine, and Kaahumanu, Lani. *Bi Any Other Name: Bisexual People Speak Out.* Boston: Alyson Publications, 1991.

Isay, Richard A. *Being Homosexual: Gay Men and Their Development.* New York: Avon Books, 1989.

Kopay, David, and Young, Perry Deane. *The David Kopay Story.* New York: Bantam, 1977.

Marcus, Eric. *The Male Couple's Guide: Finding a Man, Making a Home, Building a Life.* New York: Harper Collins, 1988.

———. *Making History: The Struggle for Gay and Lesbian Equal Rights, 1945–1990.* New York: Harper Collins, 1992.

Martin, April. *The Lesbian and Gay Parenting Handbook: Creating and Raising Our Families.* New York: Harper Collins, 1993.

McNeill, John J. *The Church and the Homosexual.* New York: Next Year Publications, 1985.

Miller, Neil. *In Search of Gay America: Women and Men in a Time of Change.* New York: The Atlantic Monthly Press, 1989.

———. *Out in the World: Gay and Lesbian Life from Buenos Aires to Bangkok.* New York: Random House, 1992.

Muller, Ann. *Parents Matter: Parents' Relationships with Lesbian Daughters and Gay Sons.* Tallahassee, FL: Naiad Press, 1987.

Pallone, Dave. *Behind the Mask: My Double Life in Baseball.* New York: Viking, 1990.

Pies, Cheri. *Considering Parenthood.* San Francisco: Spinsters, 1988.

Plant, Richard. *The Pink Triangle: The Nazi War Against Homosexuals.* New York: Henry Holt and Company, 1986.

Russo, Vito. *The Celluloid Closet: Homosexuality in the Movies.* New York: Harper Collins, 1981.

Schow, Ron; Schow, Wayne; and Raynes, Marybeth. *Peculiar People: Mormons and Same-Sex Orientation.* Salt Lake City: Signature Books, 1991.

Schulenburg, Joy A. *Gay Parenting: A Complete Guide for Gay Men and Lesbians with Children.* Garden City, NY: Anchor Press, 1985.

Sherman, Suzanne. *Lesbian and Gay Marriage: Private Commitments, Public Ceremonies.* Philadelphia: Temple Univ. Press, 1992.

Shilts, Randy. *And the Band Played On: Politics, People, and the AIDS Epidemic.* New York: St. Martin's Press, 1987.

———. *Conduct Unbecoming: Gays and Lesbians in the U.S. Military.* New York: St. Martin's Press, 1993.

Spong, John Shelby. *Living in Sin? A Bishop Rethinks Human Sexuality.* San Francisco: HarperSanFrancisco, 1988.

Uhrig, Larry J. *The Two of Us: Affirming, Celebrating and Symbolizing Gay and Lesbian Relationships.* Boston: Alyson Publications, 1984.

Vacha, Keith. *Quiet Fire: Memoirs of Older Gay Men.* Trumansburg, NY: The Crossing Press, 1985.

Van Gelder, Lindsy, and Brandt, Pamela Robin. *Are You Two. . . Together? A Gay and Lesbian Travel Guide to Europe.* New York: Random House, 1991.

INDEX